BASIC

Option
Volatility
STRATEGIES

Understanding Popular Pricing Models

BASIC

Option
Volatility
STRATEGIES

Understanding Popular Pricing Models

— WITH —

SHELDON
NATENBERG

Marketplace Books
Glenelg, Maryland

ISBN: 1-59280-344-X
ISBN 13: 978-1-59280-344-6
Printed in the United States of America.

Table of Contents

PUBLISHER'S PREFACE

What you have in your hands is more than just a book. A map is simply a picture of a journey, but the value of this book extends well beyond its pages. The beauty of today's technology is that when you own a book like this one, you own a full educational experience. Along with this book's author and all of our partners, we are constantly seeking new information on how to apply these techniques to the real world. The fruit of this labor is what you have in this educational package; usable information for today's markets. Watch the video, take the tests, and access the charts—FREE. Use this book with the online resources to take full advantage of what you have before you.

If you are serious about learning the ins and outs of trading, you've probably spent a lot of money attending lectures and trade shows. After all the travel, effort, expense, and jet lag, you then have to assimilate a host of often complex theories and strategies. After thinking back on what you heard at your last lecture, perhaps you find yourself wishing you had the opportunity to ask a question about some terminology, or dig deeper into a concept.

You're not alone. Most attendees get bits and pieces out of a long and expensive lineage of lectures, with critical details hopefully sketched out in pages of scribbled notes. For those gifted with photographic memories, the visual lecture may be fine; but for most of us, the combination of the written word and a visual demonstration that can be accessed at will is the golden ticket to the mastery of any subject.

Marketplace Books wants to give you that golden ticket. For over 15 years, our ultimate goal has been to present traders with the most straightforward, practical information they can use for success in the marketplace.

Let's face it, mastering trading takes time and dedication. Learning to read charts, pick out indicators, and recognize patterns is just the beginning. The truth is, the depth of your skills and your comprehension of this profession will determine the outcome of your financial future in the marketplace.

This interactive educational package is specifically designed to give you the edge you need to master this particular strategy and, ultimately, to create the financial future you desire.

To discover more profitable strategies and tools presented in this series, visit www.traderslibrary.com/TLEcorner.

As always, we wish you the greatest success.

Chris Myers
President and Owner
Marketplace Books

HOW TO USE THIS BOOK

The material presented in this guide book and online video presentation will teach you profitable trading strategies personally presented by Sheldon Natenberg. The whole, in this case, is truly much greater than the sum of the parts. You will reap the most benefit from this multimedia learning experience if you do the following.

Watch the Online Video

The online video at www.traderslibary.com/TLEcorner brings you right into Natenberg's session, which has helped traders all over the world apply his powerful information to their portfolios. Accessing the video is easy; just log on to www.traderslibrary.com/TLEcorner, click *Basic Option Volatility Strategies* by Sheldon Natenberg under the video header, and click to watch. If this is your first time at the Education Corner, you may be asked to create a username and password. But, it is all free and will be used when you take the self-tests at the end of each chapter. The great thing about the online video is that you can log on and watch the instructor again and again to absorb his every concept.

Read the Guide Book

Dig deeper into Natenberg's tactics and tools as this guide book expands upon Natenberg's video session. Self-test questions, a glossary, and key points help ground you in this knowledge for real-world application.

Take the Online Exams

After watching the video and reading the book, test your knowledge with FREE online exams. Track your exam results and access supplemental materials for this and other guide books at www.traderslibrary.com/TLEcorner.

Go Make Money

Now that you have identified the concepts and strategies that work best with your trading style, your personality, and your current portfolio, you know what to do—go make money!

MEET SHELDON NATENBERG

As you will learn later in this book, volatility is the most nebulous factor in determining what the value, and therefore the price, of an option actually should be—and no one is more adept at assessing volatility than Sheldon Natenberg.

As Director of Education for Chicago Trading Company and a highly sought-after lecturer at professional training seminars both here and abroad, Sheldon has helped many of the world's top institutional investors, mutual fund managers, and brokerage analysts better understand volatility and utilize it in valuing and pricing options of all types.

However, his greatest claim to fame came as the result of his authorship of *Option Volatility and Pricing: Advanced Trading Strategies and Techniques* (McGraw Hill, 1994)—considered by many to be the finest book ever written on the subject. First published in 1988 (revised in 1994), the book established Sheldon as one of the world's most acclaimed authorities on volatility and its impact on option pricing and trading strategies—a reputation he has continued to build ever since. His ongoing success at evaluating and applying option trading strategies ultimately earned him induction into the Traders' Library Trader's Hall of Fame.

What Sheldon Is Preparing to Tell You

So, why do you need Sheldon's expertise? Quite simply, because volatility has become a dominant factor in today's world—not only in the investment markets, but also in everyday life. Though this book may not enable you to understand fully the growing political, economic, and social turbulence that roils daily life, it will help you understand—and potentially profit from—the extreme volatility apparent in the financial arena over the past two decades.

In the pages that follow, Sheldon will explain the theoretical basis of volatility systematically, showing you how to calculate volatility levels in various markets, how volatility affects the price movements of different investment instruments, and how you can profit from those price movements.

He will talk about the four different categories of volatility, the differences between them, and the types that play the most important role in the leading theoretical pricing models. He will also fully describe the most popular option pricing models in use today and discuss their advantages, as well as some problems you may encounter when using them.

Specifically, he will detail the critical impact that volatility has in establishing values and prices for exchange-traded options and reveal the most common strategies for capturing the discrepancies that develop when option prices and values get out of line.

In addition, he will do it all with a minimum of mathematical equations and technical jargon.

In short, whether you've been an active trader for years or are just now considering whether to buy your first put or call, the advice Sheldon provides will prove invaluable in integrating options into your personal arsenal of investment strategies.

Chapter 1

THE MOST IMPORTANT TOOL FOR ANY OPTIONS TRADER

This book focuses on options, explaining how volatility affects the valuation and pricing of options, and how you can use this information to refine your option trading strategies and improve your trading results.

Depending on your situation, this book is a bit unusual for me because I'm used to dealing almost solely with professional traders—traders for market-making firms, financial institutions, floor traders, computer traders, and so forth. I know that you may not be a professional trader. However, lest that concern you, I'd like to assure you of one thing:

The principles of option evaluation are essentially the same for everyone.

Second, by way of disclaimer, I want to clarify something immediately: I am not going to tell you how to trade.

Everyone has a different background. Everyone has a different goal in the market ... different reasons for making specific trades. What I hope you'll at least be able to do—from the limited amount of information I'm going to provide—is learn how to make better trading decisions.

However, you're the one who must decide what decisions you're going to make.

 See Sheldon as he introduces the world of options to you. Log in at www.traderslibrary.com/TLEcorner to gain exclusive access to his online video.

Your Goal Is Not to Cut off Your Hand

Learning about options is like learning how to use tools—and everyone applies tools in different ways. For example, if somebody teaches you how to use a saw, your first question becomes, "What can I do with this saw?"

Well, depending on how well you've learned your lesson, either you can make a beautiful piece of furniture—or you can cut off your hand.

Obviously, those are the two extremes: there are many other uses in between. My point here is that I'm trying to help you avoid cutting off your hand. You may not learn enough to become a professional trader, but you will learn enough to avoid disaster, and greatly improve your trading skills.

Maybe that's not the best analogy, but I think you get the idea.

People often ask me about the types of strategies I use and which are my favorites. I think most professionals would agree with me: I'll do anything if the price is right.

The same standard defines my "favorite" strategy, because my favorite is any strategy that works—and, if the price is right, a strategy usually works.

So, how do I determine whether the price is right?

I determine if the price is right the way almost everybody does: I use some type of theoretical pricing model—some type of mathematical model that helps me determine what I think the price ought to be.

Then, whatever strategy I choose to use depends on whether the actual prices available in the market deviate from what I think they ought to be, or whether they're consistent with what I think they ought to be.

So, the primary tool for any professional option trader is a theoretical pricing model—and, if you're going to succeed with your own trades, such a model will become your primary tool as well. With that in mind, let's talk about a typical theoretical pricing model.

Black-Scholes: The Grandfather of Pricing Models

By far, the most common option-pricing tool used today is the Black-Scholes model (See Appendix B for details). Of course, there are other models that are also widely used, but the Black-Scholes model is most famous because it was the first really widely used pricing model. It was also a theoretical innovation—so much so that Myron Scholes and Robert Merton, who helped develop the model, received the Nobel Prize in Economics for its development.

So, if Merton shared in the prize, why is it called the Black-Scholes model?

Well, as a quick aside, this is a perfect illustration of the fact that life is not fair. The Nobel Prize is given posthumously only if you die within six months of the awarding of the honor. Fischer Black did much of the theoretical work in developing the Black-Scholes model—but because he died roughly eight months before the honors were announced, he missed the Nobel Prize.

Of course, his name lives on in the title of the model—and everyone who knows the story acknowledges that Black really shared the Nobel Prize with Scholes and Merton.

The Fundamental Elements of Any Pricing Model

Whether you use Black-Scholes or some other pricing model, there are certain inputs that have to be plugged into the formula. Only after you enter all of these inputs into the model you're using can you come up with a theoretical value for an option. So, let's take a look at the required inputs (Figure 1).

Most pricing models, including Black-Scholes, require five—or, in some cases involving stocks, six—inputs. If you've done any analytical work with options at all, you're likely familiar with the first four of these inputs:

- The exercise price
- Time to expiration
- The price of the underlying security
- The current interest rate

That's because these are things you can generally observe in the marketplace, as is dividend information, which is the added input stock traders are required to factor into the model. You may not know exactly what the correct interest rate is, or exactly what the underlying stock or futures price is, but you can make a pretty good guess. Likewise, if you're doing stock options, it's pretty easy to come up with the dividend. Obviously, if you're trading index options or options on futures, there is no dividend.

The big problem with almost every model, including Black-Scholes, is volatility.

It's the one input that you can't directly observe in the marketplace. Of course, there are sources of volatility data that might enable us to guess what the right volatility input is. However, we never really know exactly whether we're correct—and that's the big, big headache for all traders who use a theoretical pricing model.

Not only is it extremely difficult to determine the volatility, but traders learn very quickly that, if you raise or lower the volatility just a little, it can have a tremendous impact on the value of the option. What happens?

Either the option's value explodes, or it collapses.

Obviously, whether you're a professional trader devising hedging strategies for a mutual fund or an individual investor selecting options for a covered-writing program in your personal account, a lot will ride on your ability to determine a correct volatility input for the theoretical pricing model. You simply can't afford—in terms of either money or long-term trading success—to be at the mercy of such errors in valuation.

That's why I focus the bulk of my discussion on just what this volatility input is—what it means, how it's used, how you interpret it, and so forth.

FIGURE 1

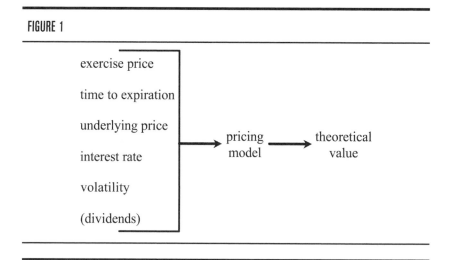

Self-test questions

1. Sheldon Natenberg's favorite options strategy is the one where the price is right. How do you determine whether the price is right?

    a. By buying in the money calls
    b. By using the right tools
    c. By using a theoretical pricing model
    d. By hedging all your trades

2. What is the most common option pricing tool used today?

    a. The theoretical pricing model
    b. The Black-Scholes Model
    c. The Myron-Merton Pricing Model
    d. The Binomial Model

3. Which of the following statements about Black-Scholes is incorrect?

    a. You should never have to calculate a Black-Scholes option value yourself
    b. There are no transaction costs
    c. Trading of the asset is continuous
    d. It uses an American-style option and can be exercised at any time up to expiration

4. What is the biggest problem, and the one unknown factor, when using pricing models?

    a. Exercise price

    b. Time to expiration

    c. Volatility

    d. Interest rate

For answers, go to www.traderslibrary.com/TLEcorner

Chapter 2

PROBABILITY AND ITS ROLE IN VALUING OPTIONS

To understand volatility and why it's so important in calculating option values, you have to understand a little bit more about how theoretical pricing models work. This doesn't mean I'm going to launch into a lengthy discussion of option theory, nor am I going to present some complex differential equation and walk you through it step by step like I might if this were a university classroom.

What I am going to do is discuss, in general terms, the logic underlying the theoretical pricing models, and use some basic examples to illustrate how they work. As we go through this process, I think you'll find that all of the models are actually fairly easy to understand in terms of the reasoning that goes into them.

For starters, Black-Scholes and all the other theoretical models that we use in determining option values are probability based. What exactly does that mean? Well, consider this:

Assume you went out and bought a stock, or you bought a futures contract. Why did you buy that particular stock? That particular futures contract? Obviously, you bought it because you thought it was going up. Were you sure it was going up? Of course not! Unless you have access to some kind of insider information, you can never be sure. All you can ever say is that the stock or futures contract will be more likely to go up than go down.

In essence, then, all trading decisions are based on the laws of probability.

Overcoming the Subjective Nature of the Process

The problem with saying that a stock is more likely to go up than down is that this is a very subjective judgment—and the theoretical pricing models don't like subjective inputs. The models say we need to assign actual numbers—specific numerical probabilities—to the possibility of the stock going up or to the possibility of the stock going down. So, how do you derive these specific numerical probabilities?

To illustrate, I've created a very simple situation. Assume there is an underlying stock or commodity that's trading at a price of 100. Then let's say that, at some future date—which we'll call "expiration"—this security could take on one of five prices, ranging from 90 to 110. I'm also assigning probability to each of those five outcomes—10 percent, 20 percent, 40 percent; then 20 and 10 again—as shown on the scale in Figure 2.

Obviously, this example is overly simplified, but it's best to start from a very simple point for the sake of clarity.

Now, suppose I go into the market and buy the underlying contract, the underlying security. If I were to ignore transaction costs, interest rate considerations, slippage—all the other real-world things we have to deal with—could I actually calculate what I might expect to get back on this contract?

The answer is yes—at least as it relates to calculating all of the likely possibilities.

Here's how it would work in this particular case. Ten percent of the time, the price of contract at expiration will come up 90. Twenty percent of the time, it'll come up 95; 40 percent of the time, it will

 To see Sheldon as he describes this example in detail, watch now at www. traderslibrary.com/TLEcorner.

FIGURE 2

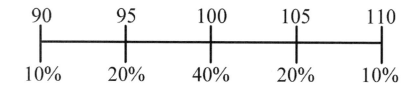

90	95	100	105	110
10%	20%	40%	20%	10%

come up 100; and so on, up to 110, where it will once again wind up 10 percent of the time. In other words, what we're doing is taking the probability that the contract will wind up at each of the five possible closing prices, and then totaling these probabilities. When we do that, you see that the total turns out to be 100. See Figure 3.

What this means is that, if the underlying contract is trading at 100 and you go in and buy that contract—or sell the contract, for that matter—the probability is that you're not going to make any money. Of course, you're not going to lose any money either—except in the form of transaction costs.

So, as professional traders, what we would say is that this contract or security is arbitrage-free—that there's no money to be made in the underlying market. At least that's what a theoretician would say.

However, it's a different story with options. Suppose that, instead of buying the underlying security, I run out and buy a 100 call.

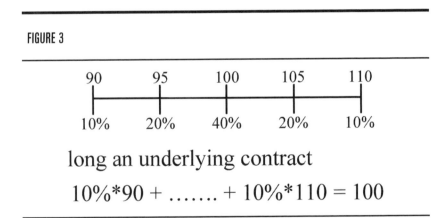

FIGURE 3

long an underlying contract

$$10\%*90 + \ldots\ldots + 10\%*110 = 100$$

How much would I expect to get back at expiration?

Forget about the price I'm paying for the call. For the moment, I'm not interested in that—or in the potential profit or loss. Right now, I just want to know what the call is likely to be worth at expiration. How do we calculate the probabilities on that? We do it in the same fashion as we did with the underlying contract—though there are some major differences.

We've already seen that the result would be a break-even with the underlying contract. But what happens with a 100 call if the un-

European vs. American Options

Most of the examples in this book refer either to the current market price of options or to their expected value at expiration. That's because Black-Scholes and the other leading theoretical option-pricing models all assume that we're dealing with European-style options. The term "European" is a distinction given to certain types of options based on the point in time at which the "right to exercise" is granted. Most options traded in Europe can be exercised—that is, exchanged for the underlying security—only on the specified expiration date. By contrast, virtually all options traded in North America (with the exception of options on stock index futures, some currency options, and a few options linked to actual physical commodities) can be exercised at any time up to and including the stated expiration date.

Options in the former class are thus referred to as "European" options, whereas those in the latter class are called "American" options. Always remember this distinction when using theoretical option pricing models to value exchange-traded options on U.S. stocks and futures contracts.

FIGURE 4

long an underlying contract

$10\%*90 + \ldots\ldots + 10\%*110 = 100$

long a 100 call

$20\%*5 + 10\%*10 = 2.00$

Expected Return

derlying contract is priced at 90, 95, or 100 at expiration? What's that 100 call worth? Zero!

You see, an option has a nonsymmetrical payoff diagram. If the underlying contract is at 100 or below at expiration, the 100 call will always be worthless. But, if the underlying contract is at 105, the 100 call will be worth 5 points. Assuming the same probabilities you saw in Figure 2, that's going to happen 20 percent of the time. Likewise, if the underlying contract is at 110, the 100 call will be worth 10, which will happen 10 percent of the time (Figure 4).

If I then add up these partial probabilities, I come out with a theoretical value for the 100 call of 2.00 points. In other words, the laws of probability say that, if I pay 2.00 points for the 100 call today, the likelihood is that I will break even on the option at expiration.

Thus, defined in simplest terms, the theoretical value of an option is what the laws of probability say will happen in the end.

Of course, there are some lesser considerations that also have to be taken into account with most of the pricing models—for example, interest rates. In this instance, if the expected return was 2.00 points and the current interest rate was 12 percent, you would have to discount the expected return by the cost of money—determining what is sometimes called the present value of 2.00 points. In this case, the interest-rate adjustment would give us a revised theoretical value of 1.96 points (See Figure 5).

In addition, there can be a substantial difference between the theoretical value and the actual market price. That's because, if I were an

---

FIGURE 5

The *theoretical value* is the price you would be willing to pay today in order to just break even.

If the expected return of the 100 call is 2.00, what is its theoretical value?

interest rates = 12%
2 months to expiration

2.00 - (2.00 x 2%) = 1.96

---

options market trader, I'd always try to bid at less than the theoretical value and offer at more than the theoretical value.

In other words, if I were a trader, somebody might come to me and ask, "Shelly, what's your market in the 100 call?" Even though the theoretical value of the call was 2.00, I would say, "I'm 1.90 at 2.10," or, "I'm 1.80 at 2.20"—whatever spread I thought I could get away with, depending on the competition in the marketplace.

If I trade using spreads such as those, does it guarantee that I'm going to make money? No, of course not. It just says that, if I do it enough times, in the long run, I should profit by the difference between my trade price and the theoretical value.

The Problem with Probabilities

So, the first step in understanding any theoretical model is to understand that all the models are based on probabilities.

The big problem comes in determining accurate probabilities.

All of the theoretical models—and, once again, they all work in essentially the same way—require that you propose a series of potential ending prices for the underlying security. That's what I did in the previous example when I set prices ranging from 90 to 110. The models then require that you try to assign a probability to each of those potential ending prices—which is what I did when I said there was a 10 percent chance the price would end up at 90, 20 percent at 95, and so on. Finally, by calculating an expected return based on those probabilities, the models come up with a theoretical value for the option.

As already noted, there are lots of different theoretical pricing models. You've got the Black-Scholes model. You've got a binomial model. You've got a wavy model. You've got some other, more exotic models. However, they all use essentially the same reasoning. The big difference is in how the various models assign the probabilities.

Some of the models use historical trading patterns to assign the probabilities, some use mathematical formulas, and others use different mathematics. But all the models have one very important characteristic in common: they all assign probabilities in such a way that, if you were to trade the underlying contract, you would always break even.

In other words, each of the recognized models assumes that the underlying market is arbitrage-free.

 Watch Sheldon explain the theoretical pricing models at www. traderslibrary.com/TLEcorner.

You Can Agree to Disagree

You do not need to agree with any of the assumptions in the theoretical pricing model. However, to be an intelligent trader—to use options intelligently—you must understand what those assumptions are.

I just said that the models all assume the underlying market is arbitrage-free—which begs a question. Have you ever bought or sold a stock or a futures contract? Sure, you have. Almost everyone has at one time or another. Well, in so doing, you've just violated the key assumption in the theoretical pricing model. Why? Because the model says you can't make money. In an "arbitrage-free" market, you're supposed to break even.

Of course, people who buy and sell stocks and futures contracts know that they can make money. If you're good at using technical analysis, fundamental analysis, market timing, or whatever, you can make money buying and selling the underlying contracts. You know it, and I know it. It just doesn't happen to be a part of the theoretical world on which these models are based.

Thus, to some extent, every trader disagrees with the model. Everybody knows the model is not a perfect representation of the real world. But we all use the theoretical pricing models anyway—except we fudge. We change them around; we use them in a way that we think makes us better traders, or that makes our trading more consistent with the real world.

FIGURE 6

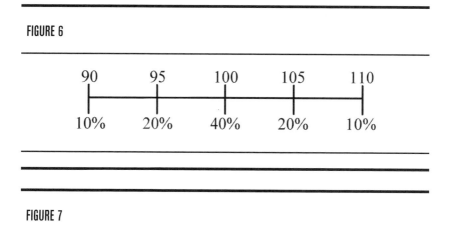

FIGURE 7

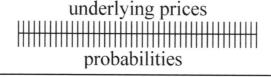

That's essentially the basis of all the theoretical pricing models.

Expanding the Realm of Probabilities

However, there's still one big problem in addition to the probabilities assigned to the prices shown for the underlying contract. The problem is that I've only proposed five potential ending prices for that contract (see the scale in Figure 6).

In the real world, how many possible prices are there for any underlying contract? That's right, an infinite number. You know, one cent, two cents, one million, two million... Just take your pick (Figure 7).

FIGURE 8

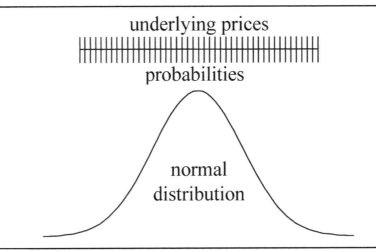

So, if I wanted to develop a really good theoretical pricing model, I'd have to consider an infinite number of potential prices, and I'd have to propose probabilities for every one of those prices.

Now, how can you deal with an infinite number of anything? Obviously, it's very difficult ... sort of like trying to count the stars in the sky. But most theoretical pricing models—traditional theoretical pricing models—have made the assumption that the world of trading looks like a normal distribution. It's the well-known bell-shaped distribution where most of the probability is located in the middle and, as you get further and further away from the middle, you have steadily declining probabilities (Figure 8).

This is reasonably consistent with our intuition about the market.

If I tell you some underlying contract is trading at 100 today, and I then tell you that, a week from now it can trade at either 101 or 1,000, which is more likely? Well, most people would say 101. Why? Because we know that, as you move further away from the current price, the probability of reaching some extreme price becomes less and less likely.

What Constitutes a Normal Distribution?

Black and Scholes were the first to make this assumption—that prices would follow a normal distribution. And, why did they make this assumption? They got the idea based on some studies that had been done on markets, dating back to the early 1900s—studies actually conducted by a French economist. The economist had reviewed the performance of some French stocks and stock indexes and came to the conclusion that, if you looked at stocks and stock indexes over a fairly long period of time, the prices did seem to be normally distributed. They did seem to form this bell-shaped curve.

Now, is this a perfect assumption? Of course not. Nobody in his or her right mind would ever say that this is a perfect assumption.

But then, Black and Scholes weren't aiming for perfection. They were trying to come up with a generalized pricing model—one that sort of fit every market, but didn't exactly fit any market.

So, this is the most basic assumption that's built into Black-Scholes and many similar theoretical pricing models—that prices are

FIGURE 9

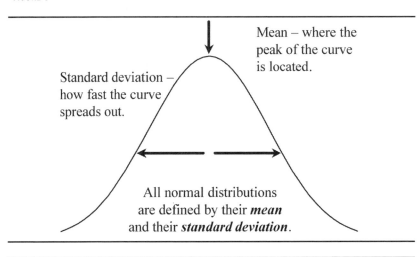

Mean – where the peak of the curve is located.

Standard deviation – how fast the curve spreads out.

All normal distributions are defined by their *mean* and their *standard deviation*.

normally distributed. The big problem for the professional or individual trader then is to determine if the market (or security) that he or she is trading really fits a normal distribution.

Earlier, I assured you I wouldn't throw up a bunch of differential equations or complicated mathematical formulas, and I also want to promise that this isn't going to turn into a course in statistics. However, to understand any talk about volatility, you simply must know a little bit more about the characteristics of this normal-distribution pattern—this bell-shaped curve.

For starters, all normal distributions are defined by two numbers— the mean and the standard deviation (Figure 9).

The mean is a measure of where the peak of the distribution curve occurs. For most purposes—just to simplify things—we assume the mean is the current price of the underlying contract.

I admit I'm fudging just a bit here on some of the theory because I don't want to make this too complex, but that definition is sufficiently accurate for most purposes.

The standard deviation is a measure of how fast the curve spreads out. Curves that have a high standard deviation spread out in a big hurry. In other words, they're very wide. Curves that have a low standard deviation don't spread out much at all; they're very narrow.

Thus, it's possible to have a number of different "normal" distributions, based on the differing means and standard deviations. Once you know the specific mean and standard deviation, the other characteristics of all normal distributions are essentially the same. Look in any statistics textbook and it will list all the characteristics of a normal distribution.

So, the mean and the standard deviation are the two numbers traders have to deal with when they're talking about volatility. We'll see precisely how they apply to volatility in a bit, but first let's see what the assumption of differing normal distributions might mean in terms of very simple option pricing.

How Distribution Assumptions Affect Option Pricing

Let's again assume that there is an underlying contract trading at 100. Now, suppose I'm interested in trading a 120 call. What is

FIGURE 10

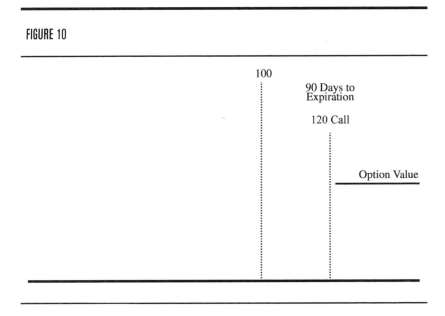

this 120 call worth? Well, the call's worth depends on, among other things, which distribution I think applies to this particular market.

Suppose there are 90 days until expiration and the value of the option depends on the likelihood of the option going into the money. In other words, it depends on how much of the assumed price distribution curve for the underlying contract is above the exercise price—or, thinking in visual terms (see Figure 10), to the right of the exercise price.

Why above or to the right of the exercise price? Because, if the price of the underlying contract is below or to the left of the exercise price, it means the call option is worth zero. At any contract price below the call's exercise price, the call is worthless.

That's one of the nice characteristics of an option—it can never be worth less than zero, no matter how far out of the money it is. Of course, what it's actually worth will depend on how much the price of the underlying contract goes above (or to the right of) the option's exercise price—that is, how much the call goes into the money.

In-, At-, or Out-of-the-Money

The most important component of an option's price, or premium—both before and at expiration—is the position of its strike price relative to the actual price of the underlying stock, index, or futures contract. All options are in-the-money or out-of-the-money at any given time—except for the rare occasion when the price of the underlying contract is exactly the same as the option's strike price. And, because many trading strategies call for buying or selling in-the-money or out-of-the-money options—or both—it is important to know which is which. By definition, an in-the-money option is one that has real—or intrinsic—value, whereas an out-of-the-money option is one that has only time value. There is, however, an easier way to make the distinction:

CALLS with strike prices below the actual price of the underlying security are in-the-money.

CALLS with strike prices above the actual price of the underlying security are out-of-the-money.

PUTS with strike prices above the actual price of the underlying security are in-the-money.

PUTS with strike prices below the actual price of the underlying security are out-of-the-money.

In addition, the put or call with the strike price closest to the actual stock price—whether slightly in-the-money or slightly out-of-the-money—is traditionally referred to as being at-the-money.

Now then, suppose I tell you that the contract underlying this call option goes up or down, on average, 25 cents every day. How likely is it that the 120 call will go into the money?

Well, without even talking about normal distributions, you probably would say: "Gee, if it goes up or down 25 cents every day, in order to get to 120, it would have to go up 80 days in a row, because 25 cents is a quarter of a point and it would have to move 20 points."

How likely do you think that is? It's almost impossible. It would be like flipping a coin 80 times and getting heads every time.

Of course, from a normal distribution point of view, we might draw the distribution curve that goes with this. Then we can easily

FIGURE 11

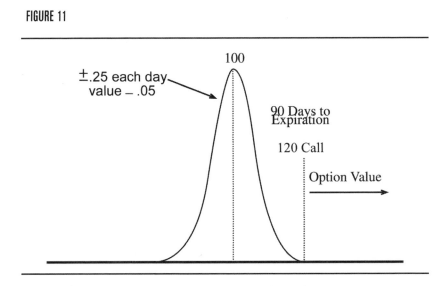

see that there's almost no chance this 120 call option will go into the money. So, given those circumstances, what's it worth now? We might give it a 5-cent value, but it's probably worth much less than that (Figure 11).

Now suppose I tell you that this market—this particular underlying contract—typically goes up or down by $2.00 every day. How likely is it that our 120 call option will go into the money by expiration? It's still not very likely because the market would have to go up by $2.00 a day for 10 days in a row before the underlying contract's price would get to 120.

If you draw the normal distribution curve that goes with this amount of daily movement, you'll quickly see that—even though

FIGURE 12

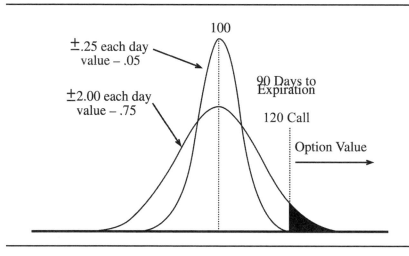

it's not very likely—there is still some chance the 120 call option could go into the money. Not a lot—but a lot more than with the 25-cent-a-day scenario (Figure 12).

A mathematician would calculate the value of this potential movement of the call option into the money, integrate the probability into a pricing formula, and then determine a current value for the 120 call. I'm not a mathematician, but I did do some quick numbers and, in this case, came up with a value of around 75 cents.

Now let's take the most extreme case imaginable for this call option: the underlying contract moves up or down by $10 every day—maybe it's a tech stock.

FIGURE 13

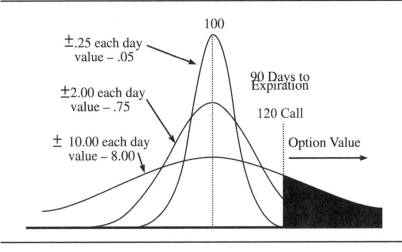

Given that, how likely is it that the 120 call could go into the money? There's a pretty good chance. That's particularly evident if you again draw a distribution curve associated with price moves of that size. The curve is much flatter and wider than in the other two cases—and a substantial portion of the curve extends to the right of the option strike price. This means that there's a good probability that the price of the underlying contract could move above the 120 strike (as represented by the black area in Figure 13). Based on that, a value of $8.00 for the option is reasonable.

So, even though in theory I might make the assumption that the market for this particular underlying security looks like a normal distribution, I still have to figure out which distribution applies before I can accurately value the call. That is obvious because, in the first case, the option was valued at 5 cents. In an alternate case, it was worth 75 cents, and in still another case it was worth 8 dollars. And you don't have to be a mathematician to know that there's a really big difference between 5 cents and 8 dollars.

The Symmetrical Nature of Distribution Curves

Review Figure 13 again. You'll notice that all three normal distributions are symmetrical. The curve to the right of the mean, or current-price line, is the mirror image of the curve to the left of the mean, or price line. In other words, the distribution looks the same moving from left to right as from right to left.

FIGURE 14

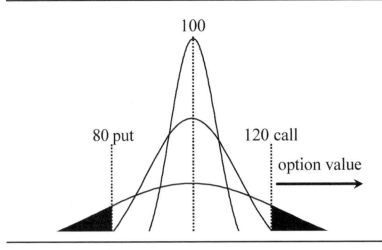

What's the significance of that in terms of option pricing?

Suppose I take an 80 put option on the same underlying security. Under what market conditions is the 80 put worth the most? It turns out the 80 put is worth the most under the same market conditions that make the 120 call worth the most (Figure 14).

That's because markets that are moving very, very quickly cause all option values to go up. The basic assumption that results from any normal distribution is that market movement is random—that you can't predict in which direction the market is going. In other words, you could say that there's always a 50 percent chance the market will go up and a 50 percent chance the market will go down.

Quite often, that turns out to be a really big surprise to new options traders, who frequently start out with the idea that what affects an option price most is the direction of the market. Of course, we quickly learn that that's not what has the greatest effect on an option's price. What has the greatest effect on the option is the perception in the marketplace about how fast the market is going to move.

So, if you get markets that are moving very, very quickly, then all options are going to go up in value. It doesn't matter whether they're puts or calls; whether they have higher exercise prices or lower exercise prices.

In the same way, if we were in a market that was moving very slowly, what would happen to all option values? They'd start to collapse—and, once again, it wouldn't matter whether they were calls or puts, whether they had higher or lower exercise prices.

Unique to the option markets is that they're very often affected to a greater extent by the perception of the speed of the market than they are by the direction of the market.

Of course, when you talk about the speed of a market, you're really talking about volatility, which we'll continue to discuss in greater depth in Chapter 3.

 Review what you've learned by watching Sheldon's online video at www. traderslibrary.com/TLEcorner

Self-test questions

1. There are a lot of theoretical models used in determining option values, but they are all based upon:

   a. The assumption that the stock market is more likely to go up than down

   b. A 20% return

   c. The subjective nature of the stock market

   d. The laws of probability

2. How do you use the laws of probability to your advantage in trading options?

   a. By assigning various probabilities that a stock will be at a certain price at a certain date and buying options that have higher probabilities of ending up in the money

   b. By assuming the stock market is more likely to go up than down

   c. By taking advantage of low probability options and cashing in big when they come in

   d. By skewing the payoff diagram to the right, thus increasing the probability of ending up in the money

3. Which option should be worth the most, given the same scenario as outlined in the chapter, that

> 10%*90 + ... + 10%*110 = 100?

a. A 100 call if the underlying contract is 90
b. A 90 call if the underlying contract is 100
c. A 100 put if the underlying contract is 100
d. A 90 put if the underlying contract is 100

4. What constitutes a "normal" distribution curve?

a. A "u" shaped chart pattern
b. A sine wave
c. A bell-shaped curve
d. The x-axis

5. All normal distributions:

a. Are made up of their mean and moving averages
b. Are defined by their mean and standard deviation
c. Peak at 100
d. Are highly volatile

6. Theoretically, what affects the value of an option the most?

a. Perceived speed of the market
b. Direction of the market
c. Whether it's a call or put
d. How many you own

For answers, go to www.traderslibrary.com/TLEcorner

Chapter 3

USING STANDARD DEVIATION TO ASSESS LEVELS OF VOLATILITY

We've now seen how probability—as it is expressed through normal distribution curves—plays a major role in determining volatility. So, how do we refine our measurement of volatility so that we can likewise refine the effectiveness of our theoretical models in valuing options?

When we talk about normal distributions, the normal distribution has certain probabilities associated with it. I'm not going to list all the probabilities—if you really want them, look in a good statistics book or probability text and you can find all the ones associated with a normal distribution. What I want to focus on here are the most important probabilities, which define what we call standard deviations.

Standard deviations are determined by dividing a normal distribution into segments. To be more precise, a standard deviation is the area under the normal distribution curve within a certain range, or magnitude, of the mean. And, that range or magnitude of standard deviation numbers is based on probabilities.

One standard deviation above the mean takes in 34 percent of all probable outcomes, and one standard deviation below the mean takes in another 34 percent of all probable outcomes. Thus, a full plus-or-minus standard deviation—one covering moves either up or down—takes in about two-thirds of all occurrences (See Figure 15). Actually, if you add 34 percent twice, it's really 68 percent. However, most people seem to find common fractions a little more comfortable, so we typically say one standard deviation takes in two-thirds of all occurrences.

We can also talk about two standard deviations from the mean, which if you add all the probabilities, takes in about 95 percent of all occurrences (47.5 percent up and 47.5 percent down). In other words, two standard deviations will cover about 19 out of every 20 probable outcomes.

Figure 16 doesn't show it, but you can also calculate three standard deviations. Of course, with three standard deviations, you're getting pretty far out. I think three standard deviations covers 369 out of every 370 occurrences, so the odds of a move of that magnitude are pretty small. I wouldn't worry too much about it.

What does all of this have to do with option pricing?

FIGURE 15

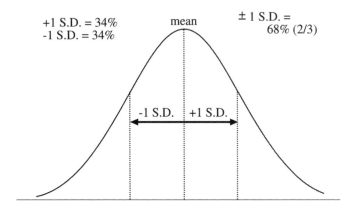

+1 S.D. = 34%   mean   ± 1 S.D. =
-1 S.D. = 34%   68% (2/3)

-1 S.D.   +1 S.D.

FIGURE 16

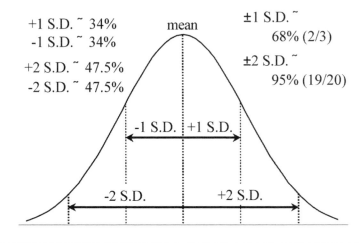

+1 S.D. ˜ 34%   mean   ±1 S.D. ˜
-1 S.D. ˜ 34%   68% (2/3)

+2 S.D. ˜ 47.5%   ±2 S.D. ˜
-2 S.D. ˜ 47.5%   95% (19/20)

-1 S.D. +1 S.D.

-2 S.D.   +2 S.D.

We've already decided that, if you're going to be a good trader, you have to use a theoretical pricing model. We've also learned that nearly all of the popular pricing models assume the world looks like a normal distribution and that the two numbers that define a normal distribution are the mean and the standard deviation. So, you have to figure out how to get the mean and the standard deviation into the theoretical pricing model.

Let's start by talking about the mean. As you saw earlier, there are five inputs that we feed into every theoretical option pricing model (six for dividend-paying stocks). Remember, we feed in the time to expiration, the exercise price, the underlying price, the current interest rate, and the volatility.

So, which one of those inputs represents the mean of the distribution? The mean equates to the underlying price—with some slight modification. I know, with pricing models, it seems there's always some slight modification. And, in this case, the modification is this: rather than being today's actual underlying price, the mean is really the break-even price at expiration for a trade in the underlying contract made at today's price.

So, what exactly do I mean by the break-even price?

Well, it's actually easier to explain if we start with futures contracts rather than with stocks. Assume for the sake of simplicity that you were to buy a futures contract at 100. If we ignore all the transaction costs and assume you hold the contract until expiration, what would the futures price have to be for you to break even? If you ignore transaction costs, margin requirements, and so forth, the answer would be 100. In other words, the break-even price is the current price.

Now suppose you bought a stock at 100 and, as with the futures contract, you held it to expiration. If the stock price were still at 100, would you break even? No, you wouldn't because of the cost of money. You had to take the money out of your account and give it to the person who sold you the stock. So, in order for you to break even, the stock would have to go up by the cost of money—by the amount of interest involved.

Of course, if the stock paid a dividend, part or all of the interest cost might be offset by the dividends received. That reflects another of those slight modifications I mentioned, one that applies only with respect to stocks. In fact, there are actually several common variations of the Black-Scholes model. There's one for stock options, one for futures options, and one for foreign currency options. They all work essentially the same way, except they calculate the break-even price slightly differently depending on interest and dividend considerations.

The term those of us in finance usually use instead of the break-even price is forward price. The forward price is simply the price that something has to be trading at on a set date in the future, such that, if you buy (or sell) it at today's price, you just break even.

 To hear more about forward prices, tune into Sheldon's lecture at www.traderslibrary.com/TLEcorner

So, for the theoretical pricing model's underlying price input we calculate the forward price and make that the mean of the distribution curve.

Standard Deviation

The other number we need to get into our model is the standard deviation. I presume you can guess what the standard deviation is: volatility. When we input volatility into a theoretical pricing model, we're simply feeding in a standard deviation. Check out the term volatility in a university textbook, and you'll find a definition such as, "the standard deviation of the rate of return." That's accurate, but it's also long, so most traders just say "volatility."

So, the volatility input for our pricing model is really just a standard deviation. The tricky part is deriving a precise definition for that volatility input. Although this is not 100 percent correct—as I said earlier, I'm fudging a little bit to keep things simple—I typically define the volatility that I'm feeding into a theoretical pricing model as one standard deviation, expressed in percent, over a one-year period.

Why do we use a yearly period here? After all, don't most of the options we trade have shorter terms of one month, two months, six months, nine months, and so forth? Yes, they do, but, historically, one year has always been the standard unit of time in financial models, and it still is. If somebody tells you interest rates are 6 percent, you don't need to ask, "Gee, is that 6 percent per month, or 6 percent per day?" Everyone knows it's 6 percent per year. You simply calculate the appropriate adjustment if you're borrowing or lending money over some other period of time.

The same is true of volatility. It's always given as a yearly number— an annualized standard deviation.

Given this definition, let's look at an example. Assume I have got an underlying contract, and we've calculated a one-year forward price of 100. And, let's also say the contract has an annual volatility of 20 percent. I won't say where this number came from. Just assume somebody gave me 20 percent.

The significance of this number to me as an option trader is that if I walk away from this contract and come back one year from now, there is a two-thirds chance that the contract will be trading within a range between 80 to 120. Why? Because 100, plus or minus 20 percent, which is the volatility—one standard deviation— creates a range from 80 to 120. And I know there's a two-thirds chance that you'll get an occurrence within one standard deviation (Figure 17).

I also know that there's a 19 out of 20—or 95 percent—chance that the contract will be trading in a range between 60 and 140 one year from now because that range equates to two standard deviations. A nice thing about standard deviations is that they're additive. If 20 percent is one standard deviation, then 2 times 20 percent, or 40 percent, is 2 standard deviations—and 100, plus or minus 40 percent, creates a range from 60 to 140.

FIGURE 17

1-year forward price = 100.00
volatility = 20%
One year from now:

- 2/3 chance the contract will be between 80 and 120 (100 ± 20%)
- 19/20 chance the contract will be between 60 to 140 (100 ± 2 x 20%)
- 1/20 chance the contract will be less than 60 or more than 140

Finally, there is only 1 chance in 20 that, if I come back one year from now, this contract will be trading at less than 60 or more than 140. That's because there's only 1 chance in 20, or 5 percent, that you'll get an occurrence in excess of two standard deviations.

Volatility Numbers Are Fluid

Now, let's look at an alternate scenario. Suppose I walked away from this contract, then came back in a year and found that the contract was trading at 180. What would you say then about the 20 percent volatility definition we've been using? Would you say it was accurate or inaccurate? Obviously, you would say inaccurate.

But, can you really be sure that 20 percent was the wrong volatility?

No, you can't. If 20 percent was the right volatility, and the market ended up at 180, how many standard deviations did the market move? Four … right on the line … but, for the sake of simplicity, we'll say four standard deviations. Twenty points—20 percent of 100—is one standard deviation, so 80 must be four standard deviations.

And, what are the chances of a four-standard-deviation occurrence? I couldn't tell you without checking a table, but let's say maybe 1 in 10,000. I don't think that's too far off. Obviously, that's a pretty outlandish number. But is 1 in 10,000 really impossible?

If you think so, then you're in for a very big surprise. In the markets, all of the things that you think can never happen because they're so statistically unlikely will eventually happen. All of them!

So, it's possible—maybe not very possible—but it's possible that 20 percent was the right volatility, and this was the 1 time in 10,000 the market did move up to 180. If it was and you were on the wrong side of the market, too bad.

Realistically, of course, I would agree that 20 percent probably was the wrong volatility because you simply don't expect an occurrence of 1 in 10,000. If I wanted to know if 20 percent really was the correct volatility, I would need to get a database of all the price moves for the contract over the last year. Then, I could put them in a spreadsheet—Excel or something similar—and actually calculate the standard deviation. Then, I might find out that the true volatility was actually 30 percent, or 40 percent. Then again, maybe I'd find that the true volatility really was 20 percent, and this was just the 1 time in 10,000 when the market was going to wind up at 180.

This is a very important lesson that all traders must learn if they hope to be successful over the long term. Even though some things are very, very unlikely, you can't ignore the possibility that they might occur. If you do, that's exactly when they will occur. It's in just such instances when traders are most likely to blow out of the market, lose a lot of money, and experience disaster.

As I keep emphasizing, everything about volatility is based on the laws of probability. There are no sure things here.

Adjusting Volatility for Differing Time Periods

We now have our working definition of volatility: one standard deviation, in terms of percent, over a one-year period.

However, most people are interested in what the annual volatility tells us about price movement over some other time period. What does it tell us about movement from month to month—or about weekly price movement, or daily price movement? In fact, I would guess that the most common time unit for active option traders is daily volatility. They want to know, "What does an annual volatility tell me is going to happen from day to day?"

Well, to translate a yearly volatility number—which is the way we get the percentage—into a volatility number for some shorter period of time, we use a fairly simple formula that's based on the fact that volatility and time are related by a square root factor. It looks like this:

$$\text{volatility}_t = \text{volatility}_{annual} \times \sqrt{t}$$

The volatility over any time period, which I've labeled "t," is equal to the annual volatility times the square root of t, where t is a fraction of a year.

Thus, if I had a three-month option—or I wanted to know the standard deviation over three months—I'd have to know what fraction of a year three months is. Obviously, it's a quarter of a year. So, the square root of one-fourth—or 0.25 is one half—or 0.50.

So, I would multiply the annual volatility by one-half and that would give me the standard deviation over one-fourth of a year.

Let's talk briefly about daily volatility. What fraction of one year is a day? Well, there are 365 days in a year. However, when we talk about volatility, we're talking about the change in price from one time period to the next. And, when we talk about time periods relative to the markets, we're talking about periods during which the price can actually change. Obviously, with exchange-traded contracts—which is what we're primarily interested in—the price can't change every day of the year. It can't change on weekends and holidays, when the markets are closed, so you have to throw those days out of the 365-day year.

Depending on where you are in the world (holidays differ from country to country), you're left with approximately 250 and 260 trading days, or daily time units, in a typical year. However, most traders assume there are exactly 256 trading days in a year because the square root of 256 is a whole number, which makes all of the daily calculations a whole lot easier.

Given these factors, a day is just 1 over 256—the single unit of a 256-day year. Then, we need the square root of that—which is just one over the square root of 256, or 1/16th. So, if I want to know what a daily standard deviation is, all I have to do is divide the annual standard deviation by 16 (Figure 18).

FIGURE 18

Daily volatility (standard deviation)

Trading days in a year? 250 − 260

Assume 256 trading days

$$t = 1/256 \quad \sqrt{t} = \sqrt{1/256} = 1/16$$

$$\text{volatility}_{daily} \sim \text{volatility}_{annual} / 16$$

This is a rule almost every floor trader knows because it's such a common calculation, and it's a rule you should also remember for your own use.

 Watch Sheldon explain this example step by step in his online video at www.traderslibrary.com/TLEcorner

Let's look at another example. We'll again assume a contract with a current price of 100, and we'll go back to my original volatility input of 20 percent. What does that tell me about the size of daily price movements I can expect?

Well, I know that to calculate a daily standard deviation, I've got to divide 20 percent by 16, which is 1¼ percent or 1.25. Therefore, I can say that if this contract closed last night at 100, then there is a two-thirds chance that, tonight, it will close between 98.75 and 101.25. Why? Because that's the range when you take 100 plus or minus 1¼ percent (100 − 1.25 = 98.75; 100 + 1.25 = 101.25).

So, in this case, 1¼ percent is still one standard deviation—but it's one daily standard deviation. And, the probability associated with one standard deviation is always two-thirds.

I can also say that there's a 19 out of 20 chance that this contract will close tonight between 97½ and 102½. Why? Well, if 1¼ percent is one daily standard deviation, then 2½ percent is two standard deviations—and 100 plus or minus 2½ percent creates a range from 97.50 to 102.50 (Figure 19).

FIGURE 19

$$\text{volatility}_{\text{daily}} = 20\% / 16 = 1\tfrac{1}{4}\%$$

One trading day from now:

- **2/3** chance the contract will be between 98.75 and 101.25 $(100 \pm 1\tfrac{1}{4}\%)$
- **19/20** chance the contract will be between 97.50 and 102.50 $(100 \pm 2 \times 1\tfrac{1}{4}\%)$

Traders are always making this type of calculation, so it's probably the standard deviation that's most common. However, if you don't trade actively or are more interested in gauging moves for longer-term positions, you can also calculate a weekly or monthly standard deviation.

You calculate a weekly standard deviation by multiplying by the square root of 1/52, which is like dividing the annual volatility by 7.2. For example, if you use our now-familiar annual volatility of 20 percent, you simply divide it by 7.2 and find that the weekly standard deviation is roughly 2¾ percent—or, to be precise, 2.778 percent. That's your weekly volatility calculation.

FIGURE 20

Weekly volatility:

$$t = 1/52 \quad \sqrt{t} = \sqrt{1/52} \quad \tilde{} \quad 1/7.2$$

$$\text{volatility}_{weekly} = \text{volatility}_{annual} / 7.2$$

Monthly volatility:

$$t = 1/12 \quad \sqrt{t} = \sqrt{1/12} \quad \tilde{} \quad 1/3.5$$

$$\text{volatility}_{monthly} = \text{volatility}_{annual} / 3.5$$

Likewise, if you are interested in monthly price movement, you can multiply by the square root of 1/12—which is like dividing the annual volatility by 3.5. Thus, with an annual volatility of 20 percent, the monthly standard deviation would be roughly 5¾ percent—or, to be precise, 5.714 percent. That's the monthly calculation (Figure 20).

Traders regularly use both of these numbers. I remind you though that the number used most often is 16. The daily standard deviation is just the most common unit of market time.

Why is it necessary to make all of these calculations? Quite simply, it's because volatility is the one thing you can't observe in the marketplace. You will always have to calculate volatility so you can enter it into your pricing model. Then, you will have to do more calculations because you'll always be trying to determine if the volatility you're using makes sense.

In other words, you'll always be asking yourself, "What do I expect to see in the marketplace—and am I seeing it?"

Examples of a Standard Deviation Conversion

We'll talk more about reviewing and adjusting our expectations in just a minute. First let's walk through another example of standard deviation conversion process.

Assume I'm looking at a stock priced at $68.50, and I think the correct volatility for that stock is 42 percent. What would be a daily standard deviation?

To find out, I take my 42 percent, divide by 16—which always gives me a daily standard deviation—and then multiply that number, which is 2.625 percent, by the stock price of 68.50. The result doesn't come out exactly, but it's very close to 1.80 (68.50 × 2.625% = 1.798), which is close enough for our purposes.

In the same fashion, I can also calculate a weekly standard deviation for this stock. Here, I would use the square root of 52 (the number of weeks in a year), which is 7.2. So, I divide 42 percent by 7.2 and get 5.83 percent. I then multiply the 68.50 stock price by that number and come out with a weekly standard deviation very close to 4.00 (68.50 × 5.83% = 3.994).

So, based on those calculations, I would expect to see daily moves within a range of plus or minus 1.80 points, and weekly moves inside a range of plus or minus 4.00 points.

Verifying Volatility

Now with the same stock at $68.50 and a volatility of 42 percent or, in daily terms, a standard deviation of 1.80—suppose this happens. I go through five trading days, and I see the following five price changes:

- Monday, the stock goes up $0.70
- Tuesday, it goes up $1.25
- Wednesday, it's down $0.95
- Thursday, it's down again—this time by a $1.60
- Finally, on Friday, it goes up $0.35

Based on that week's worth of trading, my question is, are these five price changes consistent with a volatility of 42 percent?

I'm not asking you to calculate the volatility here, because you couldn't do that without a calculator or a computer. I'm asking if, based on our discussion so far, you think these five price changes might accurately represent a volatility of 42 percent. Rather than my just giving you an answer, let's analyze the situation a bit. As you saw, if the 42 percent annual volatility that we calculated is correct, a daily standard deviation would be $1.80.

So, how often do you expect to see a price change greater than one standard deviation? Not sure? Okay, let me make it easier—I'll reverse it. How often do you expect to see a price change within one standard deviation?

That's right, two-thirds of the time. Now remember, everything in probability theory has to total 100 percent. So, if you expect an occurrence within one standard deviation two-thirds of the time, then you should expect to get an occurrence outside one standard deviation one-third of the time.

Applied to our present example, this means that, roughly one-third of the time, I should expect to see a daily price change of more than $1.80. Here are the five daily price changes again:

+ .70 + 1.25 – .95 – 1.60 + .35

How often did I see a price change of more than $1.80? None. And that seems odd because in five days you should expect to see a move outside the standard deviation at least once—and maybe even twice—because one-third of the time would be two out of six.

So, if I were trading and using a volatility of 42 percent, and I saw this kind of daily price movement, I would definitely start to consider changing my volatility. This is because if I continue using a volatility of 42 percent and keep getting price changes that aren't consistent with a volatility of 42 percent, then I've certainly got the wrong volatility.

And, if I've got the wrong volatility, then I've got the wrong theoretical values, which means my trades are not putting the laws of probability in my favor. In fact, they're probably putting the laws of probability against me.

And that, as you'll learn in Chapter 4, is something that must be corrected.

Self-test questions

1. What percent of all probable outcomes is one standard deviation of the mean?

   a. 34%

   b. 68%

   c. 47.5%

   d. 95%

2. What do those of us in finance consider the break-even point? This is also used as the mean of the distribution curve in our theoretical pricing model.

   a. The current price

   b. The current price minus any dividends

   c. The forward price

   d. The underlying price

3. Which of the following do we consider synonymous with standard deviation?

   a. Volatility

   b. A 68% return

   c. The mean price of a stock

   d. The range of a stock's price in one trading day

4. What time period is used to define volatility for most theoretical pricing models?

    a. One day
    b. One month
    c. Six months
    d. One year

5. How do you calculate a daily standard deviation?

    a. Divide the annual standard deviation by 16
    b. Divide the annual standard deviation by 4
    c. Take the square root of 365
    d. 1/256 of the annual standard deviation

6. What is the daily standard deviation of a stock priced at $40 with a volatility of 8%?

    a. 8 cents
    b. 20 cents
    c. 32 cents
    d. 40 cents

For answers, go to www.traderslibrary.com/TLEcorner

Chapter 4

MAKING YOUR PRICING MODEL MORE ACCURATE

How can you tell when you need to revise the theoretical values—particularly the volatility input—in your pricing model? Well, as you've just seen, the price movements themselves generally will provide the biggest clue.

With respect to the example I've just presented, I'll freely admit that five pieces of pricing data are a very small sampling. In the real world, when you're talking about statistics, you want to see as big a sample as possible. Typically, a professional trader might want to see price data for 20 days, 50 days, or even 100 days—certainly some larger overview of market conditions.

However, regardless of the size of your data sample, the question you must ask is always the same: What do I expect to see, and am I seeing it?

If I expect to see one thing and I'm seeing something else, then I've entered the wrong inputs into the model and have the wrong volatility.

Of course, there's a lot more to volatility analysis than just looking at the data simply because there are other real world considerations that sometimes enter the picture.

For example, after looking at the price moves just described for the stock we've been talking about, I ask if 42 percent is still a reasonable volatility estimate because, over a five-day trading period, I should see at least one occurrence—at least one price move—greater than one standard deviation. Maybe even two occurrences… But I didn't.

However, experienced traders know that when they look at data they have to analyze it, not just from a purely statistical point of view, but also from a practical point of view. Here's what I mean:

Suppose I was thinking about changing my volatility on the stock in question—lowering it from 42 percent to some smaller number that better reflected those very modest price changes, which I hadn't been expecting. I might look at the numbers one more time and, seeing nothing different, actually lower the volatility. But, on the other hand, I also might ask myself if there is any short-term reason that the market is as quiet as it is. Say, for example, that those five price changes occurred between Christmas and New Year's Day. In that case, would you suppose that they're really representative of general market conditions?

Of course not. Most traders know that people generally go home over a holiday period. They don't want to hang around an exchange or brokerage office; they want to spend time with their families. Given that, I'd probably consider that even though it was a very quiet week, I'd continue to use 42 percent because, after everyone returned from the holidays, the stock would go right back to making moves that are more consistent with my volatility input.

Thus, you can see that volatility analysis is very, very difficult. But, unfortunately, if you use a theoretical pricing model—and all good traders do—you can't ignore the volatility. You've got to think about it and try to decide on an input into your model that's reasonable.

Some Essential Adjustments to Your Volatility Input

Deciding on a reasonable input model requires making a couple of essential adjustments to your volatility calculations—adjustments that should help refine their accuracy. Earlier, I admitted I was fudging on some of the data, but I don't much want to fudge on these adjustments.

For starters, the actual volatility we feed into the theoretical pricing model is not really based on the normal distribution because a normal distribution is supposed to represent the distribution of prices in the real world. But how high can the price of a stock or commodity go? What's the upper limit? The upper limit is infinity. Obviously, it probably won't go there, but there's no law that says it can't.

I noted earlier that one important characteristic of a normal distribution is that it is symmetrical. Therefore, if I use a normal distribution, which allows prices to go up infinitely, I can expect that prices have to be able to go down infinitely, as well (Figure 21).

Unfortunately, in mathematics, negative infinity means that we have to have prices that might go below zero. However, the things we trade—traditional underlying contracts like stocks and futures—really can't go below zero. As an aside, there are some strange contracts traded in the over-the-counter market where we assign negative values but, for all the traditional exchange-traded contracts, we're bounded by zero on the downside. So, a normal

FIGURE 21

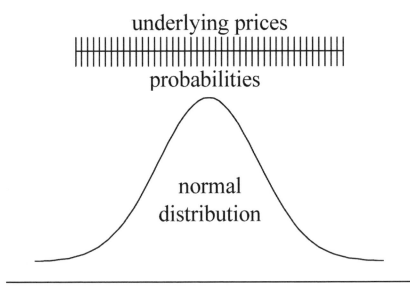

underlying prices

probabilities

normal
distribution

distribution can't really be the right distribution because a normal distribution allows for negative prices.

Thus, the actual distribution that's assumed in the theoretical pricing models is what's called a "lognormal" distribution.

Key Differences in a Lognormal Distribution

A lognormal distribution is fairly similar to a normal distribution except that it has all been pushed to the right. Also, under the assumptions of a lognormal distribution, you can't go below zero. This has to do with exponential and logarithmic functions and shouldn't concern you too much.

A lognormal distribution is very close to a normal distribution over short periods of time—but, over longer periods of time you get more upside movement. Or, to be more precise, you get a greater possibility of upside movement and less possibility of downside movement (Figure 22).

In terms of option pricing this means that we assume a lognormal distribution. Remember, a lognormal distribution says that things can go further up than they can go down.

Here's another example: Assume we have an underlying contract priced at 100—and also assume we have a 110 call and a 90 put. Now suppose that, under the assumptions of a normal distribution, the 110 call is worth 3 points. Given that we're assuming a normal distribution, the 90 put should be worth 3 points. This is because

FIGURE 22

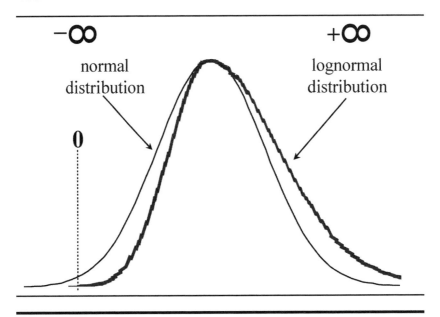

−∞   +∞

normal distribution   lognormal distribution

0

the distributions are perfectly symmetrical. In other words, there's just as a good a chance that the market is going to go up as there is that it's going to go down.

 For a full discussion of lognormal distribution, watch Sheldon's online video seminar at www. traderslibrary.com/TLEcorner

But what about a lognormal distribution? Under the assumptions of a lognormal distribution, if the 110 call is worth 3 points, do you think the 90 put would be worth more or less than 3 points?

Well, just think about it. What's the most a 110 call can ever be worth—the absolute maximum? Again, the answer is infinity—if the market can go to infinity, and does, then the call will also be worth infinity.

But, what's the most a 90 put could ever be worth? It could be worth 90 points if the market goes to zero. However, it could never be worth more than that because the market can never go below zero.

FIGURE 23

---

underlying price = 100

	normal distribution	lognormal distribution
110 call	3.00	3.00
90 put	3.00	2.50

110 call = 2.75   90 put = 3.00
Are the options mispriced?
Could there be something wrong
with the model?

Get your answer at www.traderslibrary.com/TLEcorner

Therefore, we can see that the 110 call has more room to appreciate than the 90 put because of the upside possibility. Therefore, under the assumptions of a lognormal distribution, the 90 put will always be worth less than the 110 call (Figure 23). Of course, that's based on theory, and theory doesn't have to reflect the real world.

When the Market Disagrees With the Models

You might in fact go into the marketplace and find that the 110 call is trading for 2.75 points and the 90 put is trading for 3.00 points. Does this mean the marketplace has it all wrong? Not necessarily.

Should you encounter this situation, your first step will likely be to ask if the options are mispriced. Well, if you assume the theoretical model is absolutely correct, then yes, the options are mispriced.

But, you might just as well think there is something wrong with the model.

If you've ever traded stock indexes and index options, you know this is a valid concern because you see this type of situation all the time where put prices are higher than comparable call prices. In the index markets, the downside exercise prices—the strikes we think of in terms of puts—are always inflated relative to the upside exercise prices. In other words, the marketplace generally is saying that it doesn't agree with the theoretical pricing models.

And you know what? The marketplace is probably right.

In fact, let me just ask a simple question here. Do you think the stock markets go up faster than they go down—or do you think they go down faster than they go up?

If you're like most stock traders, you said down faster than up, which means you've just disagreed with the Black-Scholes model. And you've most likely disagreed based on your own personal trading experiences—experiences that give a pretty good indication that the real world is different from the Black-Scholes world.

Indeed, if you think stock markets go down faster than they go up, then what you're really saying is that the downside exercise prices, which the market could go through very quickly, may actually have greater value than the upside exercise prices—even though the Black-Scholes model says differently.

In fact, people disagree with the model all the time. The marketplace disagrees with the model all the time. And maybe there are some very good reasons for disagreeing with the model. However, I also want to emphasize that, before you can disagree with the model, you have to understand what the model is saying and what goes into making the valuation calculations.

And, with respect to volatility, I will talk more about the subject in the following chapter.

Self-test questions

1. Which of the following may affect your theoretical pricing model?

   a. Four days of lower than average volatility

   b. A big drop in the Dow

   c. Four-day week

   d. The underlying stock moves down four days in a row

2. What is one of the real-life corrections that needs to be made to the model's normal distribution curve?

   a. Actual volatility isn't really based on normal distribution

   b. Normal distribution is asymmetrical

   c. Prices can go up infinitely but can only go down to zero

   d. Assign realistic figures for infinity and zero

3. What is the actual distribution that is assumed in the theoretical models?

   a. Implied volatility

   b. Zero to infinity

   c. Lognormal distribution

   d. Symmetrical distribution

4. In theory, using a lognormal distribution, which is worth more for an underlying contract priced at $100?

   a. 110 call
   b. 90 call
   c. 110 put
   d. 90 put

5. In the real world, why are prices higher for comparable puts than calls given that the models are lognormal?

   a. They aren't—people always disagree with the model
   b. Because stock prices are always inflated
   c. The stock market goes down faster than it goes up
   d. Because the price can go up infinitely but can only go down to zero

For answers, go to www.traderslibrary.com/TLEcorner

Chapter 5

THE FOUR TYPES OF VOLATILITY AND HOW TO EVALUATE THEM

As I've noted repeatedly, all theoretical pricing models require at least five inputs to complete the valuation formula, one of which is volatility. And volatility is the most difficult input to assess because it's the only one of the five that can't be directly observed in the marketplace. That means traders spend a lot of time talking about volatility. However, depending on the type of trading they're doing, they talk about volatility in different ways.

That's because there are different interpretations of volatility—different ways of defining volatility. Typically, traders will talk about four different forms of volatility, again depending on what they're doing in the markets.

The First Interpretation: Future Volatility

The first interpretation of volatility—one you don't hear about very much—is what we call "future volatility." This is the volatility of the underlying contract over some period in the future. Which period? Well, for me as an options trader, it's typically the period between now and the expiration of the options in which I'm interested.

If I'm trading November options, I'd like to know what the volatility—that is, the price distribution—of the underlying contract will be between now and the November expiration. If I'm trading December options, I'd like to know the volatility between now and the December expiration, and so on.

Under the assumptions of the theoretical pricing model, you can actually profit from knowing the future volatility. In fact, knowing the future volatility would be as good for an options trader as knowing the direction of the market would be for someone trading the underlying stock or commodity. Of course, I don't know the future volatility—nobody does.

Anyway, because nobody actually knows the future volatility, we have to guess what it might be. And, in trying to guess the future volatility as accurately as possible, we would need to consider other types of volatility.

The Second Interpretation: Historical Volatility

We'd probably look at the second interpretation of volatility—what we refer to as "historical volatility." This type of volatility is simply a representation of what the price distribution of the underlying contract has been in the past. By looking at past patterns, the hope is that we can make a more intelligent guess about what the future holds.

Options traders spend a lot of time looking at historical volatility. If you've ever been in a trading room at a financial institution, you know that the walls usually are covered with price charts, except when you get to the options trading section. The walls there are all covered with volatility charts. That's because we option traders are always trying to figure out what the volatility is likely to be in the future. So, we look at a lot of charts, hoping they'll help us determine that.

I'm not sure they actually do help—but it's better than making blind guesses about future volatility.

The Third Interpretation: Forecast Volatility

There are also several services and theoreticians that try to forecast volatility, providing their best guess about volatility over specific future time periods based on mathematical models.

The first volatility forecasts I ever saw were issued by Fischer Black. That was in the early days of listed options trading (I started at the

CBOE in 1982), and Fischer Black had a volatility forecasting service. He would use some model to give professional traders his best estimate of volatility over the coming three-, six-, and nine-month periods. Obviously, because he was so well known, a lot of traders subscribed to his service. However, he eventually went to work for Goldman Sachs, and I guess Goldman Sachs didn't want to share his volatility forecasts with the rest of the world because his service shut down shortly after that.

Of course, there still are numerous advisors and analytical services that try to forecast volatility. So, if you have access to a good volatility forecast, there's no reason you shouldn't use it as a tool ...make it part of your trading arsenal.

A key point here: the volatilities I've just defined—future, historical, and forecast—all are volatilities associated with the underlying contract. I haven't said anything about options yet. Thus, you can talk about the future volatility of the S&P 500. You can talk about the historical volatility of soybeans. Or you can talk about the forecast volatility for Treasury bonds. In each case, however, you are always talking about volatility in the underlying contract.

The Fourth Interpretation: Implied Volatility

There is a fourth volatility that we associate with options. This is usually called the "implied volatility," or sometimes in textbooks it's called the "implicit volatility." Almost all traders say "implied volatility."

Implied volatility is derived from the actual prices of options in the marketplace. So, what you could say is that implied volatility is the marketplace's own forecast of future volatility. It's the consensus among all traders in the marketplace about what they think the future volatility is going to be based on the prices they're currently bidding and asking for the options being traded.

How do you actually determine the implied volatility? Well, here's how it works. Let's say I want to trade an option—some specific option, it doesn't matter—and I'd like to make sure I trade that option at a reasonable price. So, I decide to use a theoretical pricing model to figure out what that option is worth.

At a minimum, I've got to feed the model the five standard inputs—exercise price, time to expiration, underlying price, the interest rate, and volatility—no matter which model I use. So, I check the marketplace for the actual values of the first four inputs and make my best guess at the volatility. I then put the data into my pricing model and come up with a theoretical value for the option—let's say I come up with a value of 2.50 points.

 What's the next thing Sheldon would do? Watch the online video for his explanation—www. traderslibrary.com/TLEcorner

Okay, if I now want to trade this option, what's the next thing I would do?

First, I need to check the price. Therefore, either I run down to the floor, call my broker, or look on my computer screen. I pick the latter alternative, pull up the quote, and it turns out this option is trading at 3.25 points!

How can I account for the fact that I think the option is worth 2.50 points, but the rest of the world seems to think it's worth 3.25?

That's not an easy question to answer because there are a lot of forces at work in the options markets that we can't really identify or quantify.

However, one method many traders and theoreticians employ is determining what causes this option to trade at 3.25 if they've made the valid assumption that the whole world is using the same theoretical pricing model.

Checking the Inputs: How to Correct Your Valuation

Let's say I'm using the Black-Scholes model, and that everybody else in the world also is using the Black-Scholes model—although that's generally not true. Nonetheless, if I believe that assumption is true, then the cause of the discrepancy has to be the inputs into the model. After all, the actual arithmetic of the model is the same for everybody.

Thus, my next step must be to go through the inputs and review the numbers. Could the problem be with the exercise price? No, we have fixed exercise prices. Could it be time to expiration? No. Assuming we can all read a calendar, that's the same for everyone. Could it be the underlying price? Well, there could be a minor problem with the underlying price because of the bid-ask spread—but in most cases the spread would never give you such a big difference, regardless of whether you entered the bid price, the ask price, or something in between. So, I say it might be the underlying price, but it's probably not. The same applies to the interest rate. Different people use different interest rates—some use borrowing rates, some use lending rates—but the differences are small. So, it's probably not the interest rate, either.

That leaves me with just one thing: the volatility. After all, it's the one thing we really can't see, the one thing that everybody has to guess about.

Okay then, let's suppose I used a volatility of 27 percent as the input in my original calculation—the one in which I calculated that the option had a theoretical value of 2.50 points. I might decide to keep these first four inputs constant. Everybody essentially agreed on those. But then I have to consider which substitute volatility do I have to feed into my model to get a theoretical value equal to the price in the marketplace.

In other words, I need to find which volatility will give me a theoretical value of 3.25.

For starters, I know that the new volatility has to be more than 27 percent because as we raise volatility, we raise the value. So, I sit down with a computer program—with my model—and I enter 28 percent, then 29, then 30. Finally, at a volatility of 31 percent, let's say I find that this option does have a theoretical value of 3.25 points.

That means that 31 percent is the proper volatility or, as we say in the market, that this particular option has an "implied volatility" of 31 percent. It's the volatility that the actual marketplace thinks is correct (Figure 24).

Do you still want to do the trade?

Given the market price and my adjusted valuation, am I still going to make a trade with this option? Well, that depends on how much confidence I have in my original volatility input of 27 percent. If I really think that's the right volatility, then I'll be happy to run in and sell this option at 3.25, because it's trading at a price way above its theoretical value.

FIGURE 24

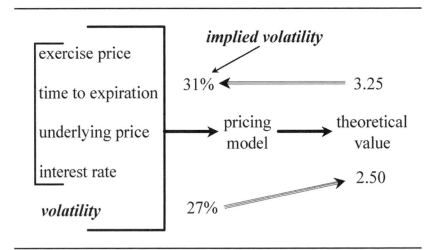

Of course, I might and probably would say that maybe the marketplace knows something that I don't. Maybe it does, maybe it doesn't. However, a basic assumption in financial theory is that markets are relatively efficient: that the prices should reflect all known information. I don't know whether this theory is true or not. I suppose if you're going to become a trader, you have to make the assumption that markets aren't perfectly efficient. If they were, you wouldn't be able to make any money trading.

I do recall one amusing story that may shed some light on the validity of the theory. At the time I was introduced to the idea of

Efficient Markets Hypothesis (EMH)

There are a number of economic theories regarding the motivating factors for security price movements, most of which pay significant attention to the causes and effects of volatility. One of the most intensely debated over the past 50 years has been the so-called Efficient Markets Hypothesis. The EMH was an outgrowth of early studies on diversification and portfolio management conducted by economists such as Harry Markowitz, James Tobin, and William F. Sharpe. Its immediate predecessor was the Random Walk Theory, which contended that security prices behaved in a manner similar to a roulette wheel, i.e. that past results had no influence on the future and could not be used to predict future price movements. In the late 1960s, this theory was extended into the EMH, which has three forms:

- The weak form, which is very similar to the Random Walk, states that current security prices fully reflect all past information and analyses of the past. Therefore they cannot provide a profitable trading strategy. This form is generally considered to be an indictment of the concepts underlying technical analysis.

continued on next page

Efficient Markets Hypothesis (cont.)

- The semi-strong form of the EMH holds that current security prices fully reflect all available public information, including that found in published financial reports. This form is generally deemed to invalidate the ideas underlying fundamental analysis, contending it is impossible to find undervalued issues based on public information. (An exception is granted in the case of insiders.)

- The strong form of the EMH contends that current security prices fully reflect all information, including that held by insiders, meaning it is impossible to predict future price movements under any circumstances.

Recent studies have noted a number of anomalies in the EMH and it has fallen out of favor over the past decade or so.

If you believe the EMH is correct that current prices fully reflect all available information and that it is impossible to predict future price movements, then you likely will want to pursue a passive form of investment and avoid the trading of options.

On the other hand, if you doubt the validity of the EMH (believing that security prices don't reflect all available information), that prices often deviate from their true value, and that astute analysts can consistently predict future price movements for underlying contracts and structure winning option positions—then you'll want to take an active approach to trading.

efficient markets, I also heard a joke that was going around the University of Chicago, which has won several Nobel Prizes in economics. It seems these two economics professors are walking down the sidewalk and one of them spots a $100 bill in the street. As he starts to bend down to pick up the bill, the other economics professor says, "Don't bother. If it were real, somebody would have already picked it up." Obviously, the second professor was a proponent of the theory that markets are always efficient, meaning there's never any free money lying around.

Of course, traders don't really believe that markets are efficient because they're still willing to trade. If markets actually were efficient, they wouldn't want to buy at the price that was asked, nor would they want to sell at the price that was offered. And neither would you.

Anyway, this is the idea of implied volatility—the only volatility based on the actual trading prices of options.

Simplifying the Volatility Assessment

Alright, we've now talked about the four different volatilities: future volatility, historical volatility, forecast volatility, and implied volatility.

If you want to simplify the situation, all option decisions begin by comparing implied volatility to the future volatility. Why? Because we equate implied volatility with the price of the option and equate the future volatility with the value of the option.

That's an absolute: it doesn't matter what you're trading, whether it's options or anything else. You are always trying to compare price and value.

If something has a high price and a low value, I want to be a seller. If something has a high value and a low price, I want to be a buyer.

And that, of course, is the foundation for all volatility-based trading strategies, which we will discuss more fully in the following chapter.

Self-test questions

1. Which of the following types of volatility is derived directly from options pricing?

   a. Future volatility
   b. Universal volatility
   c. Forecast volatility
   d. Implied volatility

2. Who or what determines implied volatility?

   a. You
   b. Historical prices
   c. The underlying price of the security
   d. The current option price

3. What is the Efficient Market Hypothesis?

   a. That security prices accurately reflect the value of their underlying companies
   b. That markets are basically efficient and price accurately reflects all available public information and it's impossible to predict future price movements
   c. That markets are efficient and therefore predictable and can be exploited
   d. That the movement of security prices are analogous to a roulette wheel and therefore create pricing imbalances that can be exploited

4. If I have figured out a theoretical value of 5 points for an option, which options price below would be my best trade?

   a. 6

   b. 5

   c. 4

   d. 3

5. Simplified, options trading comes down to:

   a. Price and value

   b. Current price versus future price

   c. Value and expiration date

   d. Price and volatility

6. If I figured out a theoretical value of 5 for an option and found it was trading at 3, what should I do?

   a. Sell the option

   b. Buy the option

   c. Double check my volatility

   d. Assume there was an error in my valuation

For answers, go to www.traderslibrary.com/TLEcorner

Chapter 6

VOLATILITY TRADING STRATEGIES

Professional traders are always looking at the implied volatility versus the future volatility. And because they don't know for certain what the future volatility is, they try to come up with an intelligent guess by looking at historical volatility and forecast volatility.

But in simplest terms, they're looking at implied volatility and future volatility—at option prices and option values.

Unfortunately, new traders very often focus only on one of these things but not on both. You can't be a successful trader that way. You can't focus on price without also thinking about value, nor can you focus on value without also thinking about price. So, there are two things involved in every trading decision.

To emphasize that point, let's look at another very quick example.

Suppose volatility in a certain underlying market has been 20 percent over the last two months, but you think the volatility over the next two months is going to be 30 percent. In other words, you think the market's going to get more volatile. What should you be doing?

Well, most new traders would think they should be buying options because when volatility goes up, then option prices go up.

That may be true, but the one thing I didn't tell you is the current prices. Maybe the marketplace also thinks volatility is going up, and the implied volatility has already risen to 40 percent. If that's the case, I'd rather be a seller of options. Even though I believe the value is going up to 30 percent, I don't want to be a buyer if the market price already is based on 40 percent. Again, I want to be a seller because the present price is higher than the future value.

So, you've got to consider both these numbers—price and value—because they both play a role in the decision process for any trade.

Now let's talk about volatility trading. That, of course, is a whole subject on its own.

The Fundamentals of Volatility Trading

Most professional traders are volatility traders. But what exactly is a volatility trade? Quite simply, it's an option hedging strategy that consists of several steps.

As a first step, you have to identify either under-priced or over-priced options—options that are mispriced in the marketplace. And, to determine whether they're mispriced, you have to determine what you think the future volatility is going to be.

In my last example, I thought the future volatility was going to be 27 percent, but I checked out the actual prices and determined that the implied volatility was 31 percent. So, the option was mispriced by 4 volatility percentage points—in this case, overpriced (assuming I was right about the future volatility).

Now remember, you want to sell things that are too expensive, and buy things that are too cheap, so you'd sell this option.

Then, as a second step in doing a volatility trade, you need to offset your initial option position by taking an opposing market position—a delta-neutral position—in the underlying security. I hope you at least understand what delta is because it's an important part of option trading. Delta measures the sensitivity of an option to changes in the price of the underlying contract. (See Appendix D: The Greeks of Option Valuation for more information about delta and other measures used in option valuation.)

The model or theory of option pricing says that you have to take an opposing market position. For example, if you buy puts on XYZ Corp., you then need to buy an appropriate number of the underlying XYZ Corp. shares. That's because a put is a short market position, while buying the underlying would create a long market position.

Likewise, if you sell an overvalued call, you also need to buy an appropriate number of the underlying shares because selling a call creates a short market position. Alternately, if you buy calls, you have to sell the underlying shares. Buying the call creates a long position; selling the underlying creates a short position. In all cases, the appropriate number of shares is the amount required to ensure that the combined positions are delta-neutral. In other words, whatever your initial action, you always take an opposing market position. However, that secondary action must be taken in a theoretically correct ratio, as determined by the delta of the option.

Further Adjustments Required

In addition, over the life of the option contact, you may have to periodically buy more of the underlying contract, or sell some of the underlying contract to maintain your delta-neutral position. This is called "dynamic hedging," or "delta-neutral hedging."

This additional adjustment is required by the volatility pricing model, which says you not only have to start out delta-neutral, but you have to remain delta-neutral throughout the life of the option.

Finally, at expiration, you liquidate the entire position at its fair value. What is the fair value? Well, for an option, it's either zero, if the option is out of the money, or the intrinsic value if it's in the money. For the underlying contract, it's the price you receive when you buy or sell at the moment of expiration.

Four Key Steps of Volatility Trading

1. Buy under-priced options, or sell over-priced options.

2. Offset the initial option purchase or sale by taking an opposing position in the underlying contract of sufficient size to make the entire strategy "delta-neutral."

3. Periodically buy or sell an appropriate amount of the underlying contract to remain delta-neutral throughout the life of the option—that is, until expiration. This is known as "dynamic hedging."

4. At the expiration of the option, liquidate the entire position.

If you do all of this properly, then the model says that, when the position is closed out, the total profit—or, if you've made a few mistakes, the loss—should be roughly equal to the amount by which the option was originally mispriced.

In theory, when the strategy is closed out, the profit (or loss) should be approximately equal to the amount by which the options were originally mispriced.

In fact, this is the method of volatility trading for which Black and Scholes really won the Nobel Prize. Most traders don't realize it now, but several variations of the original Black-Scholes model had been proposed in earlier years, so it was already possible to come up with a theoretical value for an option. What Black and Scholes did was show that you could actually capture the amount by which an option was mispriced—the difference between the option's price and its value—by going through this delta-neutral, or dynamic, hedging process.

If you're not well-trained mathematically and you look at the Black-Scholes model, it's just a long differential equation. You look at that formula and you wonder how anybody could ever make any money from that. However, most traders have learned over the years that it works fairly well.

It's not perfect, but it does a reasonably good job of predicting how you will do on a volatility trade, provided you knew the future volatility and went through this delta-neutral hedging process correctly.

Of course, it's coming up with that future volatility that's the problem.

A Black-Scholes Anecdote

To underscore that point, I'd like to recount a story I have heard that you might find interesting. It reflects how Fischer Black felt about the Black-Scholes model and this whole volatility issue (although I don't know if it's actually true).

 To hear Sheldon tell the story of Professor Black, watch the video at www. traderslibrary.com/TLEcorner

Anyway, Fischer Black was associated with the University of Chicago and, in the early days—just after the CBOE, the Options Exchange opened—traders would call and ask him about his work. Listed options were new back then, and these traders were trying to learn just how to use the theoretical pricing model.

I don't want to sound critical of Black because everything I've heard about him says he was a wonderful person who loved talking to traders because he wanted to know how his theory applied in the real world. However, one of the typical comments made about him was that he talked about volatility but didn't say what volatility he meant–whether implied volatility or historical volatility.

And Professor Black would say: "Well, what I was talking about—I thought it was obvious—was the future volatility. If you knew the volatility over the life of the option—which, of course, extends into the future—then you could go through this process and capture the difference between the price and value."

Well, most traders didn't like this answer, so typically they would ask who could possibly know the future volatility.

Black would simply reply as follows, "That's your problem. We came up with the model. You've got to figure out for yourself what to put into the model."

So, that's the problem—getting the future volatility. But, if you could get the future volatility—if you had a crystal ball and could look into the future—then you could actually capture the difference between an option's price and its value by going through this delta-neutral hedging process.

And, while most professional traders probably can't understand all the mathematics in the Black-Scholes model, they've learned through experience that it does seem to work.

If you actually are a mathematician, then maybe you can look at the equation and see exactly how it works. However, as traders, most of us base our option decisions on our real-life background and training. In truth, I guess using the Black-Scholes model is almost like a religious experience—it's a leap of faith. It seems to work. Therefore, we're going to use it. And, in real life, it does seem to work pretty well.

The Risks of Volatility Trading

Alright, we've decided that Black-Scholes seems to work, but there are quite a few risks to using it. I would divide these risks into two categories.

The first risk, which I've already mentioned, is that you've incorrectly estimated the future volatility. Obviously, that's the biggest risk for most traders because, as we've frequently heard, who knows the future volatility? Nobody.

In volatility trading, we're trying to guess the future volatility, then hedge away our risk in an option by structuring a delta-neutral position.

No intelligent options trader—no professional options trader, at least—would ever go out and take a naked volatility position. In other words, he'd never bet all his money that he's correct about the future volatility. Instead, he'll use a variety of different strategies that will remove as much of the volatility risk as possible.

So, in reality, risk elimination is what volatility trading is all about for professional traders—and failure to succeed at that is certainly the biggest risk.

Are You Naked—Or Are You Covered?

As investment strategies go, simply buying an option contract generally is considered reasonably safe because your risk is the exact amount you pay to purchase the option. You can never lose more than that.

By contrast, the act of simply selling an option is considered one of the riskiest strategies around. Sell a call option and there's absolutely no limit to how much you can lose if the underlying market goes up to infinity. Sell a put option and your potential loss is limited only by the fact that the underlying asset can't go below zero.

Because of this essentially unlimited exposure to risk, you typically are described as "naked" when you hold such short option positions.

The only way to avoid being naked—without actually buying back the option you sold—is to take an offsetting position in the underlying instrument. This is called "covering yourself"—or being covered. This process works as follows:

- If you are short a call option, you can cover yourself by buying (going long) an equivalent number of shares in the underlying stock (or other delivery units for options on other types of assets).

- If you are short a put option, you can cover yourself by selling (going short) an equivalent number of shares in the underlying stock (or other delivery units for options on other types of assets).

If risk is a significant concern in your options-trading program, don't let yourself be naked.

The second risk in volatility trading—one we don't often consider, though we really need to—is the risk that the theoretical model may be wrong.

One aspect of this that I've already mentioned is the fact that the model assumes a normal distribution. However, the real world doesn't look like a normal distribution. You've already seen an example of how this can be a huge problem in setting option prices.

In addition, there are also other problems in the model that have to do with the process of dynamic hedging. I'll just give you a quick example: As you saw at the beginning of this chapter, the theoretical pricing model assumes that you will not only structure an initial delta-neutral hedge, but that you will also re-hedge (buying or selling additional amounts of the underlying contract) as needed to keep the position delta-neutral. How often does the pricing model assume you will re-hedge the position to remain delta-neutral? Continuously!

All the assumptions in the theoretical model are based on continuous-time calculus. Of course, in the real world, you can't adjust the position continuously. That's not possible. The exchanges aren't open 24 hours a day—and, even if they were, you couldn't write the orders fast enough.

So, the fact that you can't re-hedge continuously when the model assumes that you can—or should—might cause some problems. That's an example of risk No. 2—errors in the theoretical pricing model relative to what's possible in the real world.

There are other errors in the model as well, including some that have yet to be identified. And, as option traders become more sophisticated, they focus more and more on this risk, asking about the weaknesses of the model, and what unseen threats they face if they place increasing faith in the fact that the model is right when they know that it's really not right. These are things we have to think about.

A Visual Picture of Volatility

We've talked a lot about the theoretical and mathematical representations of volatility. But what does volatility really look like? To give you an idea, I want to put up an actual volatility chart.

Figure 25 shows a roughly 12-year volatility pattern for the SPX, which is the S&P 500 Index. It clearly shows the relatively mild volatility during the prolonged bull market of the mid to late 1990s, as well as the much more dramatic volatility during the chaos that developed as the market began the topping out process and the sell-off as we entered the 21st century. That's a more extended period than what is shown on most volatility charts, but I thought

FIGURE 25

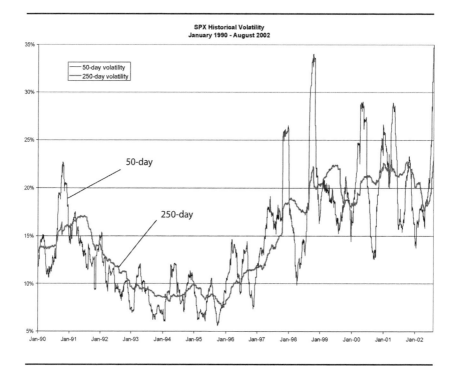

SPX Historical Volatility
January 1990 - August 2002

you might want to see how things looked over a fairly long period of time.

Actually, I put two different charts on this graphic—one showing a 50-day volatility and the other a 250-day volatility—just so I could ask this question: Which volatility line is more stable?

That would be the 250-day volatility. Obviously the 50-day volatility—the other line—is far less stable and you see tremendous fluctuations.

It's a seemingly odd characteristic to new traders that it is actually easier to predict volatility over long periods of time than it is over short periods of time.

What makes it appear odd is that usually we associate longer periods with more uncertainty. However, in terms of volatility, it's just the opposite. Now don't take this as absolute fact, but volatility is a bit like a moving average. The longer the period, the more stable the moving average—that is, the smoother the chart line. And, the same generally is true with volatility.

Of course, volatility traders know that it's a totally different story when you're dealing with short-term options. Indeed, assessing volatility over a limited period is very difficult because the volatility characteristics of the marketplace can change very quickly.

Using Volatility to Improve Your Predictions

Theoreticians try to reduce this difficulty by looking at different kinds of data and using patterns they can identify to help predict future volatility. I can't go into a great deal of depth here, but I do want to talk a bit about how this process of volatility prediction works. I suspect it's mostly an academic exercise, because I don't think you'll want to get too heavily involved in exactly how volatility forecasting models work.

To predict volatility, you need to understand some of the fundamental characteristics of volatility. Volatility is very similar to the weather. Let me give you some examples:

Suppose I told you that today's high temperature was 50 degrees, but I told you nothing else. Then I told you to make your best guess about tomorrow's high temperature. What would you guess?

If you're like most people, you'd guess 50 degrees because you know, based on real-world experience, that there is a relationship between what happens today and what happens tomorrow. In fact, even if I gave you three choices, with no other data to consider, you'd still probably guess 50.

A theoretician would describe this relationship as a "serial correlation" between the temperatures: a connection, if you will, between two consecutive events.

Serial correlations also apply to volatility. So, if I wanted to guess what the volatility over the next month would be, and I had no other data, the best approach would be to guess the same volatility we had over the last month.

Again, that's because of the serial correlation characteristic of volatility. That's not the only characteristic. Suppose today's high temperature was 50 degrees, but I also told you the average high temperature at this time of year is 45 degrees. Then I told you to choose from these three possibilities for tomorrow's high: 47 degrees, 50 degrees, or 53 degrees.

Based on the serial correlation, you might choose 50 degrees again. However, given the new information about the average temperature, it's more likely you'd choose 47 degrees. I doubt if anyone would choose 53 degrees.

Now, why would you choose 47 degrees? Because another characteristic of both weather and volatility is that things tend to return to their average. The theoreticians call this tendency "mean reversion." If the average volatility is 20 percent, but the recent volatility has been 30 percent, then there's some reason to believe that the volatility is likely to decline. Why? Because things tend to go toward their mean; they go toward their average.

There's also a third characteristic, which I'll explain this way: Let's say the high temperature two days ago was 48 degrees. Yesterday, it was 50 degrees. And, today, it's 52 degrees. What would you guess for tomorrow's high temperature: 47 degrees, 50 degrees, or 53 degrees?

Well, this one may not be quite so easy because I haven't given you any information about the average temperature. However, most people would probably guess 53 degrees because we know that temperatures tend to trend in one direction. In other words, we're in a cold wave, or we're in a warm spell. It's rarely cold one day and hot the next.

Thus, the theory is that when things start to move in one direction, there's reason to believe that they will continue to move in that direction. There is no scientific term for this, but traders generally call it "momentum": the tendency of things to continue in the direction in which they're already going. And, volatility shares this characteristic.

There are three key characteristics of volatility:

Serial Correlation—In the absence of any other data, the best guess for volatility over the next time period is the same volatility that occurred over the previous time period.

Mean Reversion—Given a past set of volatility data, the best guess for volatility is that it will return to its historical average.

Momentum—If a trend in volatility can be identified, the best guess for future volatility is that the trend is likely to continue.

Volatility has all three of these characteristics, and the theoretical pricing models currently being used will take these factors into account in their option valuations. In other words, the theoreticians will look at the average volatility, assign a reversion factor—a numerical estimate of how quickly things are likely to return to their average—and give that some weight in the pricing formula. They'll look at recent volatility and then assign some weight to the historical volatility to get the future volatility. Finally, they'll look at the direction in which volatility changes are moving, and they'll assign some weighting to that.

A Quick Look at Volatility Cones

The graph shown in Figure 26 relates to this weighting process. We often represent volatility characteristics with what are called volatility cones—sometimes also referred to as the "term structure of volatility."

These cones are used to represent the volatility characteristics of an underlying contract. The sharp curves in the lines shown on the left side of the graph depict the volatility that could occur over very short periods of time, while very flat portions of the lines on the right side of the chart represent the volatility that could occur over very long periods of time.

Notice that the general characteristic illustrated by this chart is that, over very long periods of time—in this case, three years—the volatility tends to converge. This reflects something I said earlier:

FIGURE 26

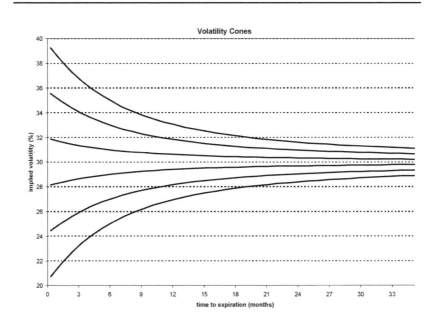

Volatility Cones

it's a lot easier to predict long-term volatility than short-term volatility. That's because, over very long time periods, the good luck and the bad luck—the high probabilities and the low probabilities—tend to even out.

So, it's a lot easier to figure out what's going to happen way over there on the right, when there's lots of time left, than to figure out what's going to happen on the extreme left, very close to expiration.

When options traders—professional trading firms—trade options, they try to come up with a term structure for volatility. That's because professional traders generally don't trade very short-term options—nothing under, say, one month. At my firm, we trade options as far out as four years.

Because of our strategy, we somehow have to be able to relate the short-term volatility to the long-term volatility, which is what the lines in the volatility cone do. That way, when we end up with lots of time spreads or calendar spreads (See Appendix C), we can say that we have a position that is consistent with the volatility characteristics of the particular underlying market.

You'll see volatility cones featured in most good options texts because it's such an effective way of representing the volatility characteristics of an underlying market. That's why I thought you should see an example of one here.

The Two Primary Models for Predicting Volatility

Another topic I want to discuss here is the two primary categories of theoretical models used for predicting volatility. Both are highly mathematical and as a result, I almost decided not to mention them here. However, they're used by many professional traders and options specialists, so you'll probably see or hear them mentioned as you seek out future volatility projections or check the results of Black-Scholes and other pricing models.

The first model or family of models is called "GARCH." That's an acronym, and nobody ever says what it stands for because it's such a tongue twister, but it stands for Generalized Auto-Regressive Conditional Heteroscedasticity.

GARCH is simply all the things I talked about earlier in this chapter.

Auto-regressive just refers to mean reversion, and the other words relate to the other characteristics that I mentioned. These models, over the last 10 years or so, have grown to be very popular. In using them, you have to decide how much weight you're going to give to the mean reversion, how much to the serial correlation, and how much to each of the other things.

Actually, it's interesting where this model came from. In the early 1960s, there was a British economist who worked for the Bank of England, and I guess the Bank asked him for a model to predict inflation in the United Kingdom to adjust money supply according to inflation.

The economist worked a while, and he came up with this model. Everybody applauded him for coming up with this model. But after all that, it disappeared—they tossed it out.

However, a decade later, when options traders were starting to think about volatility, they came across this model for inflation. Someone realized that inflation has a lot of the same characteristics as volatility and that the model could be applied to predicting volatility.

And that's what they did, though with a slightly different name. The original model was actually called "ARCH," and then generalized to "GARCH" when they started to work with options.

The other category of models isn't quite as widely used, maybe because it comes from physics rather than from mathematics. But it's also known by the acronym "VARIMA," which stands for Vector Auto-Regressive Integrated Moving Average.

Again, auto-regressive simply refers to mean reversion (you see that in everything), and the other characteristics of volatility also are factored in, though the weighting formulas are somewhat different. I doubt whether you'll come across this very often, so I won't give any more details. However, you may sometimes hear the theoreticians talk about it.

That covers at least the surface of all of the most important strategic elements involved in actually structuring and implementing volatility trades. You've seen how they're put together: what you have to do initially to put on a delta-neutral position, how to re-hedge during the life of the trade to keep it delta-neutral, and when to liquidate it. You've also learned about the difficulties in determining the correct volatility level for your trades and the primary characteristics of volatility, which can be helpful in trying to make your volatility forecasts. Plus, you've seen the two categories of models that are used most often to weight those characteristics and actually predict future volatility.

Margin Requirements and Commissions

Because it seeks to capture discrepancies between option values and their actual prices, volatility trading typically has a very small profit differential. In other words, you can't make a lot of money in absolute terms unless you deal in fairly large quantities. You also need to be very precise, taking into account any expenses that might reduce that profit differential. Commercial option trading firms and full-time professionals are able to bypass or sharply reduce many of these expense factors. However, individual traders typically can't because they have to factor such elements as commissions and margin requirements into their trade decisions.

With respect to commissions, the general rule is to look for rates as low as possible. Be aware, however, that lowest is not always best. In other words, a low commission is no good if you get slow executions, bad prices, and lousy (or no) service. So, when it comes to commissions, make sure your trading firm gives you everything you want and need to conduct your option trading program successfully even if it costs a few dollars more.

Because the options used in volatility trading should always be covered, they typically don't require a margin deposit. However, because volatility trading is so demanding, most individuals usually engage in other option strategies as well—and some of them do have margin requirements. For example, strategies such as the "naked" sale of a call or put can carry risks far in excess of the actual cash needed to initiate them, so the option exchanges mandate that traders doing these strategies deposit extra cash (or securities) with their brokerage firms to guarantee they'll meet the obligations imposed by the strategies. This collateral varies from strategy to strategy, based on the option exchange's assessment of the position's relative risk. And, it must remain on deposit for the duration of the trade, which creates an added cost-of-money (or interest rate) consideration for traders.

If brokerage firms feel the relative risk is higher than that perceived by the exchange, they may demand larger deposits. However, no firm may require less than the exchange minimum. Should the market move against a trader holding such a position, causing a loss, he or she may receive a margin call requiring the deposit of added funds to bring the collateral up to maintenance level. Failure to meet such a call could result in forced liquidation of the margined position.

You should also be aware that brokerage firms may require a substantial initial deposit just to open a trading account, just to ensure that you have enough money available to meet potential future margin requirements and trading expenses. Most firms require a minimum initial deposit of $5,000 to $10,000 to open an account—more if you plan to engage in higher-risk strategies or trade in large volumes. Thus, the opportunity loss on this money also must be factored into your overall trading results.

1. What should you do if you think volatility is going to go down by 10% on an option?

   a. Sell the option

   b. Buy the option

   c. Check the implied volatility of the option's current price

   d. Recheck your calculations to figure out why your numbers are different from everyone else's

2. What is delta?

   a. A measure of the sensitivity of an option to a change in interest rates

   b. A ratio that compares the change in the price of an option to a corresponding change in the price of the underlying asset

   c. A measure of the rate of decline in the value of an option over time

   d. A gauge of an option's sensitivity to the implied volatility of the underlying asset

3. What is the first step in trading an options hedging strategy?

   a. Offset an option position by taking an opposing market position in the underlying security
   b. Assume a delta-neutral position
   c. Identify mispriced options in the marketplace
   d. Adjust your theoretical model for current market conditions

4. What is the big key to trading an options hedging strategy?

   a. Forecasting future volatility
   b. Perfecting your theoretical model
   c. Accurate trading data
   d. Measuring the rate of decline in the value of an option over time

5. Is it easier to predict long- or short-term volatility?

   a. Long
   b. Short
   c. Neither — Time frame does not affect volatility

6. How does momentum apply to options?

   a. That options tend to return to their average volatility

   b. That options tend to continue in the directions they're already going

   c. Given no other data, momentum tends to pull prices to the previous period's level

   d. Good options traders tend to get better and bad option traders tend to get worse

7. What is the main objective of a calendar spread?

   a. Profit from sharp moves in the underlying stock

   b. Hope the underlying stock will fall or remain stable

   c. Play shorter-term option valuation against longer-term volatility

   d. Profit from the widening of the spread

8. What type of option trading strategy is the most risky and most likely requires a margin account?

   a. Straddle

   b. Hedge

   c. Naked

   d. Calendar

For answers, go to www.traderslibrary.com/TLEcorner

Chapter 7
THEORETICAL MODELS VS THE REAL WORLD

Several times, I've talked about the fact that the option pricing models might not be correct. In fact, everybody knows the models are not correct. And, as I've also mentioned, the biggest reason for that problem is that the real world doesn't look like a normal distribution.

To emphasize this more clearly, I actually took all of the historical data that I compiled in creating the 12-year S&P 500 volatility chart I discussed earlier in Figure 25, and created a histogram, which is merely a visual representation of the actual occurrences versus the theoretical occurrences.

The vertical bars in the aforementioned histogram reflect the actual occurrences in terms of the amount of movement and the number of days on which this movement occurred. The theoretical world that is assumed in the Black-Scholes model—which is derived from the data underlying those vertical lines—is represented by the linear curve overlaying the vertical lines (Figure 27).

So, how does this demonstrate that the theoretical world differs from the real world? The answer, as reflected in this histogram, is twofold:

- First, by looking at the vertical lines in the center of the chart, you can see that in the real world I'm getting a lot more days with small moves than is predicted by a normal distribution.

- Second, even though it's hard to see, on the outside edges of the chart, you can see what are called the outlyers—which represent days on which there were much bigger moves than are predicted by the theoretical pricing model.

This is a very important problem that applies to almost every market, not just to the S&P. There are always bigger moves—sometimes extremely large moves—in the real world than are predicted by any theoretical pricing model.

I can give you a perfect example. After the October 1987 crash, I sat down and calculated the volatility for the S&P for the entire year. It came out to be about 32 percent. Now, if the annual standard deviation is 32 percent, what would a daily standard deviation be? What would we have to divide by? Sixteen. And 32 percent divided by 16 is 2 percent.

So, a daily standard deviation for the S&P 500 in 1987 is 2 percent. And, do you know how much the market fell on October 19, 1987?

FIGURE 27

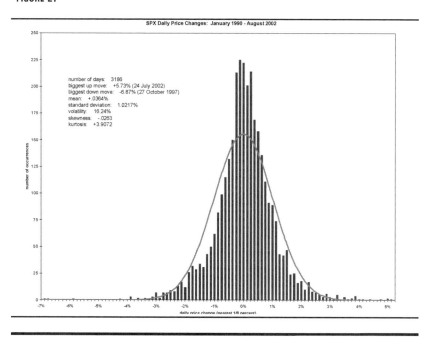

SPX Daily Price Changes: January 1990 - August 2002

number of days: 3186
biggest up move: +5.73% (24 July 2002)
biggest down move: -6.87% (27 October 1997)
mean: +.0364%
standard deviation: 1.0217%
volatility: 16.24%
skewness: -.0263
kurtosis: +3.9072

Depending on which index you look at—from 20 to 22 percent!

For the sake of simplicity, let's just say 20 percent. And, if our daily standard deviation is 2 percent and the market fell 20 percent, how many standard deviations did the market fall? Ten.

Do you have any idea what the probability is of a 10-standard-deviation occurrence? I sure don't. Just try to calculate it on your computer, and you'll just get underflow. Statistically, it's not going to happen in the history of the universe.

You may say that's an extreme example. But the fact is, things do happen in the real world that the statistical models say aren't possible. You must remember this when you're planning your volatility trading strategies—or any other option strategies, for that matter.

Summary

You can't always believe what the models tell you. When you lose money on a trade and can't figure out why, you must consider the possibility that the model is wrong. It's as simple as that.

Practice your options craft, work with the pricing and volatility models, and use what they tell you. But don't take the results they give you as gospel. Factor in your own real-world experience and observations as well. You'll be a far better trader if you do.

 To learn more, log on at www.traderslibrary.com/TLEcorner and watch Sheldon's video presentation.

Self-test questions

1. What are outlyers?

    a. Data that falls outside the curve

    b. Histogram bars that are higher than the predicted model

    c. Price movement greater than that predicted by the theoretical price model

    d. Data that fall within the curve

2. If your daily standard deviation is 3% and your option fell by 15%, how many standard deviations did your option fall from the mean?

    a. 3

    b. 4

    c. 5

    d. 6

3. Which statement is false?

    a. In the real world statistically impossible things occur

    b. You can rely upon your theoretical model

    c. You need to work with prices and volatility models in order to use what they tell you

    d. You must correct your options model to include real world occurrences

4. Using a real world example, on October 19, 1987 the Market fell by 20%, which was a standard deviation of 10 for the year. How statistically probable was this?

    a. 2%
    b. .5%
    c. .002%
    d. Less than .002%

For answers, go to www.traderslibrary.com/TLEcorner

Appendix A
OPTION FUNDAMENTALS

If you're a bit rusty on the basics and would like a modest refresher course, simply keep reading. What follows is a highly condensed primer describing what options are, how they work, general pricing guidelines, and some comments about elementary strategies.

Though options have been around in one form or another for several centuries, the modern era of options trading didn't begin until 1973, when standardized equity options were first introduced by the Chicago Board Options Exchange (CBOE). At that time, contracts were available on less than three dozen stocks, and trading was conducted in crowded pits by shouting floor brokers using hand signals and paper confirmation slips. Today, standardized options are available on more than 1,000 stocks, indexes, currencies, futures, and other vehicles; nearly 5 million equity options trade on an average market day. Well over 90 percent of those transactions are done electronically, with orders matched by computer and trades completed in a matter of seconds.

In other words, thanks to increased experience, improved computer technology, and electronic market systems, option trading has become fast, efficient, and relatively low cost—even for individual investors. But for those who've had only limited exposure to options and the arenas in which they trade, we'll review some of the basics.

What exactly is an option? Though there are a few variations, the basic definition is this:

An option is a contract giving the buyer the right, but not the obligation, to buy or sell an underlying asset at a specific price on or before a certain date. An option is a security, just like a stock or bond, and constitutes a binding contract with strictly defined terms and properties.

As securities, options fall into a class known as derivatives. A derivative is a financial instrument that derives its value from the value of some other financial instrument or variable. For example, a stock option is a derivative because it derives its value from the value of a specific stock. An index option is a derivative because it derives its value from its relationship to the value of a specific market index, such as the S&P 500. The instrument from which a derivative derives its value is known as its underlier or underlying asset.

By contrast, we might speak of primary instruments, though the term "cash instruments" is more common. A cash instrument is a security or index whose value is determined directly by markets. Stocks, commodities, currencies, and bonds all are cash instruments.

Regardless of what the underlying instrument is, there is one absolute regarding options: there are only two basic types (or classes). They are:

CALLS—A call option gives its owner the right to BUY the underlying security at a specific price for a limited period of time. In the case of equity options, the purchaser of a call receives the right to buy 100 shares of the underlying stock at the option's stated strike price. As a rule, purchasers of call options are bullish, expecting the underlying stock's price to rise in the period leading up to the option's specified expiration date. Conversely, sellers of calls are usually bearish, expecting the price of the underlying stock to fall—or, at the least, remain stable—prior to the option's expiration. However, there may be other reasons for selling calls, such as the structuring of strategies like spreads.

PUTS—A put option gives its owner the right to SELL the underlying security at a specific price for a limited period of time. With equity options, the purchaser of a put receives the right to sell 100 shares of the underlying stock at the option's stated strike price. Buyers of put options generally are bearish, expecting the price of the underlying stock to fall prior to the option's stated expiration date. Conversely, sellers of puts usually are bullish, expecting the price of the underlying stock to rise—or at least remain stable—through the option's expiration date. However, there might be other reasons for selling puts based on the objectives of certain strategies, such as lowering the cost basis on an intended eventual purchase of the underlying stock.

As the previous descriptions should make obvious, there are certain terms unique to options—terms that primarily describe the specifics of each individual option contract. To define these terms, let's assume you just bought a January 55 J.C. Penney Company call option at a price of $4.50.

- The underlying stock (or index)—This is the security that the option gives you the right to buy or sell. In this case, 100 shares of J.C. Penney Company, Inc. common stock.

- The strike price (also called exercise price)—This is the guaranteed price at which you can "exercise" your option (the price at which you can buy or sell the underlying stock). In this case, the price at which you can buy 100 shares of J.C. Penney stock is $55 per share.

- The expiration date—This is the date when your option expires (the date after which you can no longer buy or sell the underlying stock at the strike price). Options on stocks in the U.S. officially expire on the Saturday following the third Friday of the expiration month (although trading stops at the market close on the third Friday). Thus, this J.C. Penney call would expire on the third Saturday in January.

- The premium—The premium is simply the price you pay to buy an option, quoted on a per share basis. (The seller of an option gets to keep the premium, regardless of whether the option is ever exercised.) In this case, the premium was $4.50 per share, or $450 for the entire 100-share option contract.

Although they are traded as separate and unique securities, the essence of every option lies in its underlying asset, be it 100 shares of common stock, a leading market index, a foreign currency, a commodity futures contract, or any other item of value.

The importance of this link cannot be overstated if you hope to be successful as an options trader. That's because the characteristics of the underlying security will determine both the premium you pay (or receive) for the options you trade and the odds of your success with the strategies you choose. For example, assume you've been following a stock that has traded in a range of, say, $35 to $39 per share over the past six months. Obviously, options on that stock would be poor candidates for a strategy requiring either a $5-per-share price move or a rise above $40. And, if you wanted to sell options on that stock, you'd be unlikely to get premiums high enough to make many strategies worthwhile. (The example below discusses how option premiums are determined.)

Likewise, if you were interested in doing a stable-market option strategy, your odds of success would be very low if you tried it on a highly volatile market index or on a stock that had traded in a range from, say, $35 to $75 during the past six months.

Key Elements of an Option Premium

The price a buyer pays when he purchases an option—or receives when he sells one—is known as the premium. The buyer must pay the full premium at the time of the purchase (option premiums are not marginable), and the seller gets to keep it regardless of whether the option is subsequently exercised.

Equity option premiums are quoted on a per-share basis. Thus, a quoted premium of $3.75 represents an actual payment of $375 on a standard 100-share stock option contract.

The actual size of the premium for any given option is determined by a number of factors—but, in non-mathematical terms, the three most important are:

- The strike price of the option relative to the actual price of the underlying asset, which is known as the intrinsic value.
- The length of time remaining prior to the option's expiration date, which determines what is called the time value.
- The degree to which the price of the underlying asset fluctuates, referred to as the volatility value.

A basic, non-mathematical formula for option pricing could thus be:

> Intrinsic Value + Time Value + Volatility
> Value = Option Premium

Unfortunately, the only absolute in that equation is the intrinsic value. To illustrate, assume QRS stock was trading at $48 per share and you purchased a November QRS call with a $45 strike price, paying a premium of $5.50 per share. The intrinsic value of the call would be $3.00 a share—always the difference between the actual stock price and the call's strike price. (By contrast, a $50 call would have no intrinsic value because its strike price would be above the actual stock price, while a $50 put would have an intrinsic value of $2.00 per share—again, the difference between strike price and actual stock price.)

The remaining $2.50 of the $5.50 call premium would be attributed to a combination of time value and volatility value. There's no simple way to determine an exact breakdown of the two—though there are complicated mathematical formulas, typically using the Black-Scholes option-pricing model or variations thereof. As a refresher, two basics apply:

1. The more time remaining until the option's expiration, the greater the time value portion of the premium.

2. The greater the volatility of the underlying asset, the higher the volatility portion of the premium. Thus, in our November QRS example, time value would likely dominate the non-intrinsic portion of the premium in August, while volatility value would be a greater consideration in early November, after most of the time value had eroded.

Your Goals Help Determine Your Choice of Strategies

As noted earlier, options are among the most versatile of investment vehicles. They can be used for the most aggressive of speculations—and for purely defensive purposes. They can be used to produce large one-time profits, or to generate a steady stream of income. They can be used in the riskiest of investment pursuits, or specifically to insure against risk. They can be used when markets rise, when they fall, or when they fail to move at all. They can be used by themselves, in conjunction with other options of the same or different type, in combination with their underlying securities— even with groups of essentially unrelated stocks.

In fact, there are at least a score of distinct investment strategies using options alone—and another dozen or so using options in association with other securities or underlying assets. So, how do you select the right strategy?

Obviously, the goals you hope to achieve using options will dictate the strategies you employ. If you expect a major market move and your desire is to reap maximum speculative profits, then you'll likely pick the simplest and most direct of the option strategies: the outright purchase of a put or call, depending on your views about the direction of the move.

If you expect a more modest price move but still want to seek speculative profits, then you might take a more conservative approach, choosing a vertical spread using either puts or calls, again depending on whether you are bullish or bearish. If you expect a major price move but aren't sure about the direction, you may opt to position one of the more exotic strategies, such as a straddle or strangle. If you own a stock and need to generate more income from your holdings, you might add an option to the mix and write a covered call. Or, if you own a large selection of stocks and want to protect yourself against a market downturn, you could choose to buy puts on a broad-based stock index.

In short, the strategic possibilities—like the potential profits offered by options—are virtually unlimited. Whatever your specific goal, you likely can find a way to achieve it using options—assuming, of course, you are correct in your assessment of what the underlying market is going to do and that you structure your option strategy properly.

The following section discusses one element that can have a major impact on your strategy's success—choice of striking price.

Strike Price Positions & Strategic Risks

The choice of option strike price relative to the underlying stock price is a significant consideration when deciding exactly how speculative you want to be in buying options:

CONSERVATIVE—As a rule, the purchase of an in-the-money option represents the most modest speculation. Although it carries the largest premium, and is therefore most expensive in absolute-dollar terms, the in-the-money option actually is less risky because it requires the smallest stock price move to reach the break-even point and begin producing a profit. The stock also must make a sizeable move against you—enough to carry the option out of the money—before you suffer a total loss. On comparably sized price moves, real-dollar profits are larger on in-the-money options than on at-or out-of-the-money options. However, because of the higher cost, the percentage return on a profitable trade usually is lower.

MODERATE—The at-the-money option purchase provides the most balanced speculative play. The cost, and therefore the maximum risk, is moderate—as is the size of the stock-price move required to reach the break-even point and begin producing a profit. However, any adverse price move—or even a stable market—typically will result in the option expiring worthless, giving you a total loss. Dollar profits generally aren't as large, but percentage returns are higher than with in-the-money options.

AGGRESSIVE—The most blatant speculative purchase utilizes the out-of-the-money option. Although the premium, and thus the real-dollar risk, is low, the stock can move almost a full strike-price level in your favor—and you'll still suffer a total loss. And, an even larger move is needed before the trade starts making a profit. But, because of the small dollar outlay, when you do get one right, the percentage returns are quite spectacular.

Exit Strategies and Money Management with Options

Regardless of the option strategy you use, one rule always applies: Any time you implement a new trade, immediately plan an appropriate exit strategy.

This means setting both a specific loss limit and an anticipated target profit for every trade you do. It also means designating those benchmarks based on solid reasoning and sound market logic—not raw emotion. If you dislike such firm guidelines and start looking for ways to work around them, you're almost certainly headed for eventual trading failure, if not outright financial disaster. And remember, while you can give your profit targets some flexibility to allow for the pursuit of added gains, your loss limits should be absolute!

Another issue you should address in any options trading program is money management. Failure to properly apportion and control your capital can cause severe disruption—or even termination—of your trading program, regardless of the investments involved. However, with options or any other high-risk trading vehicle, a lack of clear goals and precise strategic objectives can spell disaster. Here are some of the most common mistakes you should strive to avoid:

- Trading based on emotion rather than on fact, which can lead to irrational or panic-driven decisions—and potentially devastating losses.

- Trading too much, thereby reducing the quality of your positions and increasing transaction costs.

- Initiating trades for which you're not mentally suited—that is, trades that keep you awake at night.

- Using strategies you really don't understand—then being surprised by the unanticipated outcome.

- Taking profits too soon—and holding your losing trades too long. With respect to the latter mistake, you should never be afraid to take a loss. Even the most successful option pros don't make money on every trade. So be willing to get out of a bad trade as soon as you recognize it. That's the first step in finding the next good opportunity.

- Losing too much too soon on too few trades, thereby leaving yourself with insufficient capital to make a later recovery.

- Taking advice from the wrong people, including the talking heads on TV who have an instant analysis for every minor market move.

Fortunately, if you start out with a solid plan, then do your homework before (and during) each of your trades, you can avoid most of these mistakes and develop into a competent—and successful—trader.

That covers the basic elements of options and the various ways they are traded, plus some fundamental tenets regarding risk and money management. Obviously, the information here is just the tip of the options iceberg. A far more sophisticated theoretical level is contained in the body of this book.

Leading U.S. Exchanges

If you're going to be an active options trader, it's probably a good idea to know who's handling your orders—and your money. Although nearly 95 percent of options trades now are completed electronically, the leading options markets in North America still have distinct identities and a physical presence—the exception being the International Securities Exchange (ISE), the nation's first totally electronic options marketplace. Here is a brief overview of the five major U.S. option-trading arenas:

- Chicago Board Options Exchange (CBOE)—The CBOE originated the trading of listed options in the United States, introducing a slate of standardized call options on just 16 underlying stocks in April 1973 (listed put options didn't come along until 1977). Currently, the CBOE lists options on more than 700 stocks, bonds, and market indexes and boasts an average daily trading volume of more than 1.25 million contracts. The CBOE accounted for 35.6 percent of all U.S. option trades in 2004—a total of 320 million contracts—more than 95 percent of which were completed electronically.

- American Stock Exchange (AMEX)—The AMEX, based in New York, was organized to handle the trading of stocks too small to be listed on the New York Stock Exchange. It expanded into options soon after the CBOE introduced listed contracts and now accounts for about 14 percent of U.S. options trading volume. The AMEX allows trading in more than 1,400 different options, including those listed on all other major exchanges.

- Pacific Exchange (PCX)—The Pacific Exchange is the third most active options exchange in the world, trading options on more than 800 individual stocks and a number of indexes. The PCX is a leader in electronic options trading, handling roughly 95 percent of its trades electronically—72 percent of which are processed automatically, with orders typically filled in under five seconds. Based in San Francisco, the PCX options exchange accounted for nearly 15 percent of U.S. options volume in 2004.

- Philadelphia Stock Exchange (PHLX)—The PHLX was America's first organized stock exchange, founded in 1790, and remains a highly active trading arena. More than 2,200 stocks, 900 equity options, 10 index options and 100 currency options trade on the PHLX, which handles around 6.2 percent of U.S. options volume.

- International Securities Exchange (ISE)—The ISE has experienced overwhelming growth since its founding in 1997. Though it started slowly, with just 1 percent of the nation's trading volume in 2000, it has since exploded and now handles about 30 percent of U.S. option trades. Its interlinked computer network can provide up to 1 million quotes per second and is capable of matching buy and sell orders and confirming completed trades in five seconds or less.

Note: Options are also traded on the Montreal Stock Exchange, the Toronto Stock Exchange, and the Canadian Venture Exchange (in Vancouver), but listings are primarily for Canadian stocks.

A BASIC LOOK AT BLACK-SCHOLES

Every advisory service that specializes in option strategies, as do all of the leading brokerage firms, has the Black-Scholes theoretical option pricing model (along with several alternative models) programmed into its data analysis computers. Thus, it's unlikely you will ever have to personally plug numbers into the formula and calculate whether an option you're considering is over- or undervalued. Still, if you're going to put your hard-earned dollars on the line based on what the model says, you should at least know what Black-Scholes looks like.

The formula is actually presented in a couple of different ways: one, using Greek letters and mathematical symbols and, the other employing the standard Arabic alphabet. However, since formulae filled with Greek letters tend to ignite the math phobia in many people, we'll stick with the Arabic version. In that format, the basic Black-Scholes formula for evaluating the price of a call option looks like this:

$$sN(d1)\text{-}e\text{-}r(T\text{-}t)XN(d2)$$

where:

s is the price of the underlying security

$N(x)$ is the cumulative standard normal distribution of x

e is the mathematical constant

r is the risk free rate of return

X is the exercise price of the option

T is the time of expiry of the option

t is the time now

z is the volatility of the option

d1 is $(1/(z\sqrt{(T\text{-}t)})(\ln(s/X)+(r+ z2/2)(T\text{-}t))$

d2 is $d1 - z\sqrt{(T\text{-}t)}$

In addition to these inputs, the Black-Scholes model makes the following assumptions:

- The option is a European option—that is, it can only be exercised at the option's maturity date.

- There are no transaction costs.
- The risk-free rate is known and constant over the life of the option.
- The volatility of the price of the underlying asset is constant over the life of the option. The formula in essence assumes that the size of the next move in the asset's price is known, but the direction is not. There are no "jumps" in the asset's price.
- The asset does not pay dividends.
- Market prices are arbitrage-free.
- Trading of the asset is continuous (i.e., the stock market is always open).
- Fractions of the asset can be traded (i.e., half a share can be purchased).

Obviously, some of those assumptions are unrealistic in the real world, but they are generally deemed acceptable for determining theoretical values. There are several ways of deriving Black-Scholes prices using this formula and these assumptions, but even the easiest is a bit too mathematical to cover here. Thus, if you want a more detailed explanation, you should refer either to my book, *Option Volatility & Pricing: Advanced Trading Strategies and Techniques*, or to any other comprehensive options text.

The Black-Scholes formula does have some weaknesses, the biggest resulting from the assumption that probabilities for future prices of the underlying security follow a normal distribution. This is an approximation that is good enough most of the time, although it may not be precise enough for those engaging in arbitrage or doing ultra-short-term, high volume trades seeking to capture very small margins. Still, for the average options trader, it is one of the most effective and readily understood option pricing tools.

Appendix C

CALENDAR SPREAD:
Putting Time on Your Side

Professional option trading firms use many advanced strategies to profit from both price moves in the underlying assets and inconsistencies between option values and prices. One of the most popular is the so-called "calendar spread," also known as a time spread. With the advent of LEAPs (Long-term Equity Anticipation Securities) and other extended-term options in the 1990s, many variations of this strategy—based on complex mathematical equations—became possible. However, all the variations rely on the same basic concept, which is implemented by the following:

- Selling—or going short—a near-term option contract
- Simultaneously covering that short position by buying (or going long) an option of the same type (put or call) on the same underlying asset with the same striking price, but with a more extended expiration date

For example, if it were January and your pricing model indicated the April 50 call options on XYZ stock were overvalued, you might sell those options short and cover your position by simultaneously buying July 50 XYZ calls—that is, calls with the same striking price but an expiration date three months further out.

There are two possible objectives for a calendar spread. The first is to profit from the widening of the spread, or difference, between the prices of the two options—a widening that inevitably will occur as the near-term option (the one you sold) approaches expiration and begins to rapidly lose its time value. This will always happen, assuming there is no move in the underlying stock sufficient to carry the options deep into or out of the money, thereby sharply diminishing the time value in the prices of both options.

Many traders turn this strategy into a serial trade, buying an option with a truly extended expiration date—say, two to three years out—then repeatedly selling a new near-term option as soon as the prior one expires. By doing this, they can capture the time-value decay in a whole series of expiring options while having to buy only one longer-term covering option. Remember that this strategy can be crippled by sharp moves in the underlying stock since such moves reduce the time-value component that makes the process worthwhile.

The second objective is more speculative in that you hope the underlying stock will fall or remain stable (in the case of a call spread) until the near-term call's expiration date, then rise sharply while you are still holding the longer-term option. If this occurs, the call you sold will expire worthless—or you'll be able to buy it back at a low cost—and you'll then make a sizable profit on the longer-term option when the stock rebounds. Most traders (especially professionals) opt for the more conservative approach, content to take the small, but relatively sure profit that results from the inevitable time-value decay. However, the other approach is a reasonably low-cost way to speculate on a large future price move in the underlying stock.

Note: Calendar spreads are effective only where the options involved are cash settled (such as on the major market indexes) or call for delivery of the same underlying asset, such as shares in a common stock. They don't work in most futures markets, where options on the same commodity call for delivery of different underlying contracts. For example, March corn options call for delivery of March corn futures, while June corn options call for delivery of June corn futures. Thus, the prices don't correlate perfectly.

Appendix D

GREEKS OF OPTION VALUATION

Delta is one of five analytical tools known collectively as "The Greeks," so-called because four of the five are named after letters of the Greek alphabet. The exception is "Vega," which, for reasons unknown, was named after the brightest star in the constellation Lyra. (Note: At times, Vega has also been called "kappa," but the name Vega is now generally accepted.)

Traders use the Greeks to measure risk in portfolios containing options because of exposure to certain variables—specifically the price movement of an underlying instrument, implied volatility, interest rates, or time. The Greeks are defined individually as follows:

Delta—A ratio that compares the change in the price of an option to a corresponding change in the price of the underlying asset.

Gamma—A measure of second-order option-price sensitivity to the movements of the underlying instrument. More precisely, gamma measures the rate of change for delta as the underlying asset price moves closer to or further from the option's striking price. If an option is deep in-the-money or deep out-of-the-money, the gamma is very small. If an option is at-the-money, the gamma is at its largest.

Vega—A gauge of an option's sensitivity to the implied volatility of the underlying asset. Specifically, Vega measures the change in an option's price compared to a 1 percent change in implied volatility, which rises or falls when there are large movements in the price of the underlying asset. Vega tends to diminish as the option nears expiration.

Theta—A measure of the rate of decline in the value of an option over time; also referred to as time-value decay. All options will lose value as the expiration date for the option draws nearer. However, theta is not actually considered a measure of risk because the passage of time is certain and therefore entails no theoretical risk.

Rho—A measure of the sensitivity of an option to a change in interest rates. More precisely, Rho is a measure of the rate of decline in the value of an option over time. Also referred to as "time decay" on the value of an option. The option will lose value as the maturity of the option draws closer.

There is another term named after a Greek letter—beta—that is also used to measure the movement of assets, primarily in the equity markets. Specifically, beta measures a stock's volatility in relation to the broad market. That is, it tells us if a stock is more or less volatile than the S&P 500. If a stock has a beta of 1.00, it means it usually moves in precise step with the overall market. A beta greater than 1.00 means the stock's price movements will be more volatile than those of the total market, whereas a beta below 1.00 means the share price will be less volatile than the market. Though beta has no direct application to options, it can be useful in assessing an underlying stock's risk, which affects the implied volatility of related option contracts.

Appendix E
KEY TERMS

Black-Scholes – Fischer Black and Myron Scholes are considered the founding fathers of Quantitative Finance for their ground-breaking work, published in 1973, in deriving a formula for the pricing of options and other corporate liabilities. Not only did their pricing model specify the method for pricing listed stock options, but it also laid the foundation for the pricing of most other derivative financial instruments, leading to substantial growth in their acceptance and use over the past three decades. Specifically, the Black-Scholes option pricing model is designed to value European-style (exercisable only at expiration) put or call options on a stock that does not pay a dividend, assuming the underlying stock price follows a geometric pattern with constant volatility. In practice, rather than deriving the specific price of a given option, which is actually determined by market supply and demand, the model most often is used to compute the implied volatility of the option.

Deviation – A statistical measure of the historical volatility of a security, portfolio of securities or derivative instruments related to those securities. More specifically, the standard deviation of a security is the extent to which its price can be expected to move up or down from its present level during a given period of time. The deviation of a given security can be represented visually by a so-called distribution curve. For example, securities that have a very high standard deviation are evidenced by distribution curves that spread out rapidly from the peak or "mean" (usually the current price), while those that have a low standard deviation have curves that are very tall and narrow.

Distribution – The range of potential prices a security or derivative instrument, such as an option, might be expected to reach over a given period of time. The most likely price outcomes define the so-called "standard deviation," while more extreme outcomes are measured in multiples of the standard deviation. Prices outside the range of normal expectations, though not impossible, generally are considered to be so unlikely as to be excluded from a so-called "normal distribution."

Distribution Curve – A visual representation of the range of expected prices for a security or option over a given period of time. In the case of stocks or other perpetually trading securities, the distribution normally takes the shape of a classic bell curve. In other words, it peaks in the middle (at the current price, or "mean"), then follows a uniform curve that becomes flatter and flatter as it moves outward to the extremes on both sides of the mean. Distribution curves for options tend to have an upward bias (for calls) or a downward bias (for puts) because the distribution possibilities on the opposite side are limited by the option's striking price.

Forecast Volatility – One of the four basic interpretations of volatility. A prediction, or "best guess," regarding the degree of price movement, or volatility, that can be expected for a given security in the future. With respect to derivative securities, such as options, forecast volatility usually relates to the predicted price movements of the underlying asset rather than of the option itself.

Future Volatility – This is the volatility of an option's underlying contract over a specific future time period—typically the period leading up to the expiration of the option being evaluated. While future volatility is always an estimate, such estimates are important in determining the level of time value appropriate in an option premium.

Historical Volatility – This is generally considered to be the most accurate assessment of volatility since it merely reflects what the price distribution of an option's underlying security has been in the past. By looking at past patterns, the hope is that one can make a more intelligent guess about future price movement. Option traders spend a lot of time studying historical volatility, as represented by graphic illustrations known as volatility charts.

Implied Volatility – The fourth and, for option traders, most important form of volatility. Also sometimes referred to as "implicit volatility," implied volatility is derived from the actual prices of options in the marketplace. In other words, implied volatility is the marketplace's own forecast of future volatility—the consensus among all current option traders regarding what they think the future volatility is going to be, based on the prices they're currently bidding and asking for the options being traded. The true value of the Black-Scholes option pricing model, rather than being the determination of the price of an option, lies in its ability to assess implied volatility.

Lognormal Distribution – A lognormal distribution is very similar to a normal distribution except that the pattern of potential prices has a slight upside bias. This is because, under the assumptions of a lognormal distribution, the price of the subject security cannot go below zero. Thus, the long-term pattern must allow for the possibility of slightly more upside movement and slightly less downside movement. However, over shorter periods of time, there is very little difference between the normal distribution and lognormal distribution.

Mean – A measure of where the peak of a security's distribution curve occurs. For most purposes, it is assumed that the mean is the current price of the security—or, in the case of options, the current price of the underlying contract.

Options – An option is a contract giving the buyer the right, but not the obligation, to buy or sell an underlying asset at a specific price on or before a certain date. Options fall into a class of securities known as derivatives, which are financial instruments that derive their value from the value of some other financial instrument or variable. For example, a stock option is a derivative because it derives its value from the value of a specific stock. There are only two basic types (or classes) of options:

- Calls give their owners the right to buy the underlying security at a specific price for a limited period of time. Purchasers of call options generally are bullish, expecting the underlying stock's price to rise in the period leading up to the option's specified expiration date. Conversely, sellers of calls usually are bearish, expecting the price of the underlying stock to fall—or at least remain stable—through the option's expiration date.

- Puts give their owners the right to sell the underlying security at a specific price for a limited period of time. Buyers of put options usually are bearish, expecting the price of the underlying stock to fall before the option's stated expiration date. Conversely, sellers of puts usually are bullish, expecting the price of the underlying stock to rise—or at least remain stable.

Pricing Model – A mathematical formula designed to factor in a range of variables—such as time, implied volatility, etc.—that affect the price of a given security or portfolio of securities and thereby calculate what the value of that security or portfolio should be. With respect to options, the best known and most widely used pricing model is the Black-Scholes model (see Black-Scholes, above).

Probabilities – Mathematical percentages assigned to a given situation to estimate the likelihood that the price of a specific stock or option will wind up at a given level at a specified point in the future (e.g., in the case of options, this is typically the expiration date). For example, if a stock is trading at $100 a share, you might assign a 30 percent probability that the stock would wind up at a price of $90 a month in the future and a 30 percent probability that it would end up at $110. Prices at a greater distance from the current price—say $80 or $120—would be assigned a lower probability. The total of all probabilities, when plotted on a graph, create what is known as a distribution curve.

Theoretical Value – Though adjustments must be made for a number of variables—such as the level of the striking price relative to the current price of the stock—the theoretical value of an option is, in simplest terms, the value that the laws of probability say will likely be achieved in the long run (i.e., by the expiration date).

Valuation – The process by which a fair price is determined for a security, index, portfolio, or derivative instrument. There are a variety of methods for assessing valuation, ranging from theoretical pricing models (such as Black-Scholes) through fundamental and technical analysis to purely market-driven assessments based on what buyers are willing to pay and sellers are willing to accept for the transfer of the asset.

Volatility – The degree to which a security, option or other trading instrument is likely to move up or down from its current price. Historical volatility and expected future volatility are major factors in determining the amount of time value appropriate in the price of any given option.

Volatility Assessment – The process of evaluating the four types of volatility, factoring in other pricing elements such as striking price and time to expiration, and using this data to uncover disparities between an option's current trading price and its actual value.

Volatility Trading – A multi-step option hedging strategy that begins by identifying options that are mispriced in the marketplace, then buying those that are under-priced and/or selling those that are overpriced. As a second step, you then offset your initial option position by taking an opposing market position—a delta-neutral position—in the underlying security. For example, if you bought an under-priced put, you would also buy an appropriate number of shares in the underlying security (i.e., a put is a short market position, while buying the underlying stock would create a long market position). Finally, over the life of your volatility trade, you would periodically buy (or sell) shares of the underlying security as needed to keep the entire position delta-neutral (a process known as "dynamic hedging"). The goal of volatility trading is thus to create a risk-free position that will capture the disparity between an option's inaccurate market price and its true value.

Index

NOTE: Figures are indicated by "f" following the page number. Page numbers for definitions of key terms are in boldface.

at-the-money calls and puts, 25, 124

auto-regressive, 101

M

margin calls, 104

margin requirements and commissions, 103–5

market condition and option price, 30–31

market disagreeing with pricing model, 64–65

mean of a distribution pattern. *See also* standard deviation

as break-even price at expiration, 38–39
normal distribution, 22–23, 22f
overview, **144**
mean reversion aspect of volatility, 95–96, 98, 101, 102

Merton, Robert, 4

mispriced options. *See also* volatility trading

and calendar spread, 133–35
identifying, 85
market contradicting analysis, 64–65
recovering the difference between value and price, 87–88

moderate options trading, 124

momentum aspect of volatility, 96–97

money management, 125–26

monthly time units, 49

moving averages, 95

N

naked trade risks, 90, 91–92, 104

normal distribution

curve (*See* normal distribution curve)
flaw of negative side, 59–60
lognormal distribution vs., 61
overview, 21–23, 22f
as pricing model assumption, 19–23, 20f, 22f, 92, 131–32
S&P 500, 12-year volatility chart showing variance in, 93–95, 94f, 109–12, 111f
variations based on security movement, 26–29, 26f, 27f, 28f
normal distribution curve

applying information to, 26–29, 26f, 27f, 28f
overview, **142–43**

and standard deviation, 23,
36, 37f
symmetrical nature of, 29–31,
30f

O

options

calendar spread trading,
133–35
calls (*See* call options)
distribution curves for, **143**
expiration date, 13, 70, 118,
120–21
history and quantity of trades,
115–16
and implied volatility, 73–74,
75–80, 76f
importance of underlying
asset, 119
and market conditions, 30–31
mispriced (*See* mispriced
options)
nonsymmetrical payoff
diagram, 13–15, 14f,
15f
overview, 116–18, **144–45**
premiums, 118–19, 120–21
pricing (*See* option pricing)
puts (*See* put options)
seller's risk, 91
terminology unique to
options, 118–19
trading principles (*See* also
volatility trading)

underlying assets (*See*
underlying assets)
universal trading principles, 1
versatility of, 122–24
option premium, 118–19, 120–21

option pricing. *See* also pricing
models

and distribution assumptions,
23–29, 24f, 26f, 27f,
28f
and future volatility, 83–84
and implied volatility, 79–80,
83–84
and symmetrical nature of
distribution curve,
29–31, 30f
option value and future volatility,
79–80

outliers, 110, 111f

out-of-the money calls and puts,
25, 124

P

Pacific Exchange (PCX), 128

Philadelphia Stock Exchange
(PHLX), 128

potential prices, assigning value
to, 16–17, 19–21, 20f. *See*
also probabilities

premium, 118–19, 120–21

position, 85–86
dividend-paying stocks as, 5,
    38, 39
and forecast volatility, **143**
and future volatility, 70, 79–80,
    143
for offsetting initial option
    position, 85–86, 91–92
overview, 118, 119
price of security as mean in
    normal distribution, 23
price of security as pricing
    model input, 5
and probability of potential
    outcomes, 10–12, 11f,
    12f, 19–21, 20f
and serial trades, 134–35
trading range with annualized
    volatility rate, 41–43,
    42f
volatilities associated with, 72
underlying price, 4, 38–39, 74–75

U.S. exchanges, 127–28

V
valuation. *See also* probabilities

actual market price vs.
    theoretical value, 15f,
    16
determining theoretical value
    of call options, 13–15,
    14f, 15f
interest (*See* interest)

intrinsic value, 120–21
option value and future
    volatility, 79–80
overview, **146**
of potential prices, 16–17,
    19–21, 20f
strike price and option value,
    28–29
theoretical value, 6f, 15, **146**
time value, 120–21
time-value decay, 134, 138
volatility value and premium
    amount, 120–21
value and price, 28–29, 83–84

VARIMA (Vector Auto-
    Regressive Integrated
    Moving Average), 102

Vega, **138**

verifying volatility, 51–53

volatility

as annualized standard
    deviation, 40–44, 42f
assessment (*See* volatility
    assessment)
characteristics of, 95–97
daily time units, 45–48, 46f,
    48f, 50–51
forecast volatility, 71–72, **143**
future (*See* future volatility)
historical (*See* historical
    volatility)

This book, along with other books, is available at discounts that make it realistic to provide it as a gift to your customers, clients, and staff. For more information on these long lasting, cost effective premiums, please call us at (800) 272-2855 or you may email us at sales@traderslibrary.com.